The American Myth and the European Mind

STUDIES IN
AMERICAN CIVILIZATION

Department of American Civilization
Graduate School of Arts and Sciences
University of Pennsylvania

THE ANGLO-AMERICAN CONNECTION
IN THE EARLY NINETEENTH CENTURY
by Frank Thistlethwaite

THE AMERICAN MYTH AND THE EUROPEAN MIND
by Sigmund Skard

The American Myth and the European Mind

AMERICAN STUDIES IN EUROPE 1776–1960

by

Sigmund Skard

Professor of Literature, especially American, University of Oslo

Philadelphia
University of Pennsylvania Press

Preface

THE impact of the United States on Europe is an aspect of modern life which long has had a strong appeal to Europeans. In comparison, the problem has much less interested the Americans themselves. Up to recent times the average citizen of the United States was apt to be overawed by the civilization of the Old World and to think modestly of the contributions of his own nation. Even today, the idea that the United States has exerted much influence outside its own borders is not generally held in America. On a recent ocean crossing, the writer told an elderly American journalist from one of the newspapers in New York that he holds a full chair of American literature at a university in Norway. The journalist gulped a few times and then whispered with an apologetic smile, "Oh yes, Longfellow!" Even the young American summer school students in postwar Oslo, when told about the strong American strain in Norwegian history, often listen with surprise.

Beginning with the First World War, however, and much more so after the Second World War, the importance of America beyond its boundaries gradually began to be recognized on both sides of the ocean. Today, the rôle of the United States in the life of mankind is obvious, and even the Americans are increasingly made aware of it, by their taxes if not otherwise. Appreciation of the American impact is indispensable to an objective understanding of the modern world. And gradually this interest has also come to include America's rôle in Europe's past. These studies are only in their beginnings, and their results are uneven. But already we clearly see their relevance and their potential importance, particularly to the intellectual history of Europe itself.

The immediate object of research has been, of course, the palpable connections between the two worlds—diplomatic and military contacts, political intercourse, economic ties, immigration. In these fields we have by now at least an over-all picture. Behind these contacts there were the more devious influences of American civilization, for instance, the European acceptance or rejection, meekly or passionately, of the manifold products of American life, from sewing machines and movies to books and ideas. Here we know a good deal less. And beyond these piecemeal reactions there is an even more general and much less tangible impact, namely that of the United States as an entity. In the 1780's the Frenchman Crèvecœur wrote about America's "close affinity with our present time"; and what he said about the 1780's continues to be true. The life that developed in the Western Hemisphere proved to represent a lasting intellectual challenge to the world. The image of the United States carried a vicarious value, positive and negative; while depicting America it came at the same time to serve and to reflect, in a curious and revealing way, the needs of the Europeans themselves.

Here research is very much in its beginnings; yet we know enough to see that it holds high promise. Investigation of this field is bound to teach us important things about the history of popular and public opinion. The growth and development of the image of America in Europe, the continuous adoption or repression, combination or re-creation of stereotypes—these offer fresh insight into the myth-making imagination of the Europeans. Many of their hopes and dreams, hatreds and fears through the ages have used Amer-

ican symbols, lending the image of the United States a strange
and independent life of its own. In the words of a Dutch
scholar, "The myth about America which we cultivate in
Europe has a psychological reality which is much more important to us than the so-called truth about America."
But this is only one part of the process. From the very beginning, this myth-making, with its touch of the emotional
and the sensational, ran parallel with serious efforts on the
part of the Europeans to make America into something else,
not only a vehicle of dreams but an object of sober understanding. These tendencies often were mixed, or they worked
at cross purposes; but the distinction is real enough. Since
the discovery of America, there has been in Europe an urge
to test the American symbols, to check the dream against the
reality (because there *is* something like an American reality),
to sift the myth through the critical, scholarly, skeptical mind
as part of an intellectual conception of the world.

The building up of such serious understanding has been
the task of what in this book is called American studies in
Europe. This term does not refer to the speculations of arm-
chair philosophers or the stray observations of travelers. Nor
does it include, for instance, European studies of American
geology or flora and fauna, however careful. It equally ex-
cludes the adoption by Europeans of American methods of
research, say in chemistry or logic or psychology, a process
that is important but that has little to do with America as
such. "American studies" is taken to mean the efforts to
build up a systematic knowledge and understanding of America and its civilization as a connected whole, particularly in
those fields—human geography, history, politics, law, religion, language, and literature—which constitute a national
culture. Such efforts, of course, cover a wide range; among
others, they include the entire field of independent scholar-

ship. But of necessity they have their nuclei in the universities, the natural centers of intellectual life, where research is organized and knowledge accumulated and passed on, and in the secondary schools, where that knowledge is divulged and digested and made a part of the heritage of the nation.

This subject has really, in the words of the poet, been "swaddled with darkness." With regard to scholarship pure and proper, some beginnings have been made. (One could mention as an outstanding example Eugene E. Doll's book on German historians of America from 1770 to 1815, published in 1948 by the American Philosophical Society.) But when it comes to the history of organized American studies in European schools and universities, research amounts to practically nothing. The only general survey to appear was an anonymous British article published in 1873, which evenly mixed facts and fancy and was justly forgotten. And the general assumption seemed to be that such American studies, as far as they existed, had only originated after the Second World War.

When the author of the present book took up this problem for investigation some years ago, it was for strictly practical reasons. But he soon discovered that more American studies were going on in Europe than anybody imagined. And this experience was duplicated as the present efforts were traced back to their beginnings. What originated as an administrative report thus ended as a general history of the systematic study of the United States in European secondary schools and universities in the period from the American Revolution to the present time as part of the interrelations of the Old World and the New (*American Studies in Europe: Their History and Present Organization*, 2 vols.: University of Pennsylvania Press, Philadelphia, 1958). The book was one of a series of publications of the American Institute of the University of Oslo.

This investigation was based on research at many universities and libraries throughout Western Europe. It was supported generously by American authorities, and no less by the helpfulness of European colleagues. This notwithstanding, the scope of the work was limited by the very nature of the sources involved. The survey of academic requirements, for instance, had to rely largely on printed regulations, regardless of the fact that practice may often have been different. The history of teaching had to refer almost exclusively to specialized work; what has been included of American materials in courses on general subjects usually could not be ascertained, although such courses may often have been of greater importance than those where America was explicitly mentioned in the title. Even within these limits the task was beset with difficulties. Thousands of lecture lists had to be patched together from incomplete and war-devastated libraries in many countries; and even if the findings were supplemented by extensive research in other sources, in particular by extensive correspondence and discussion with hundreds of scholars and educational authorities, many problems still had to be left unsolved. But the main outlines emerged clearly enough.

These general results were presented, in the Fall term of 1957–58, as a series of lectures, which the author gave as a visiting professor of American Civilization at the University of Pennsylvania; the following spring he repeated the series at the University of California (Berkeley) and the University of Wisconsin. While the bulk of the material presented in these lectures is to be found in the two volumes referred to above, it was added to in the oral presentation and was arranged from a different point of view, making it generally more accessible than it could be in a documented analysis. On a number of points it has later been possible to bring this survey up to date, paying attention to the rapid growth within the subject itself.

In the preface and the acknowledgments of my *American Studies in Europe* I have thanked the many institutions, informants, and collaborators who made my investigation of the subject possible. In the notes and other references in that book I have also given an extensive account of my sources as far as they appear in print. I now express my gratitude to the University of Pennsylvania, which first invited me to give these lectures, and to the University of Pennsylvania Press, which wished to publish them. I thank my friends Charles and Mary Boewe for their delightful co-operation in preparing the manuscript for publication, and most of all my colleague, adviser, and friend through many years, Professor Robert E. Spiller, who has followed and furthered my American studies with active interest from their very beginning.

Oslo, Norway; December 1960.   Sigmund Skard

Contents

The American Myth and the European Mind

1. In Revolutionary Fervor (1776–1865)

THE story of how the nations of the world, large and small, have studied each other through the ages is one of the most thrilling chapters in the history of civilization, because the motives are so manifold. The development of such studies is only in a technical sense the concern of pedagogy. It is a part of the international give and take of cultural values. It is determined by factors of geography and history, by the heritage of traditions and the immediate needs of the day, and by the orientation of the nations toward the entire world—as Leopold von Ranke said, "by their special relation to God." And this complexity is particularly striking with regard to the United States because of its special position among the nations.

To Europe the New World always had an air of the strange and fantastic. Even the small British colonies on the East Coast early shared in this atmosphere of the extraordinary, as demonstrated, for instance, by the first European descriptions of the paradisiac city of Philadelphia. And from the Revolution on, these hopes were fulfilled beyond any expectation. The dreams of the Old World came to life in the New. The free states of North America gave the signal for the greatest political and social upheaval in European history. They inaugurated an economic and technical growth which was to be envied and imitated by the world. They fascinated the Europeans by a civilization which proved to have unexpected and universal appeal. And by mass immigration this

New World came to be linked to the Old and to the broad layers of its population in a way that lacked any parallel in history.

Thus, even in the eighteenth century, and increasingly in the nineteenth, serious American studies might seem to have been a matter of obvious concern to all Europe. But there were also other factors at work. There were practical difficulties. America was far away. It took time to get there, and travel and transportation were expensive. News was largely secondhand; and there was little material with which to check it. Few Americans realize the poverty of American source material in most research libraries in Europe before 1945, or even now.

Neither have American studies always been regarded as too desirable by those in power. America came to symbolize the forces of change; but these forces faced a solidly conservative and traditionalist Europe that came back in strength each time it was challenged. The governing classes had little use for American republican ideas, less for the social equality of the new states, and least of all for America's dubious cultural offerings, which often were felt to be coarse and provincial, similar to the "uncultivated" sound of American English to European ears.

The recognition of American values was bound to be particularly slow in European education. Far into the nineteenth century schools and universities in the Old World were the stronghold of the classes in power and of their ideals. Politically conservative and socially selective, these schools were old-fashioned in their methods, and centered their curricula mainly around the heritage of classical antiquity. In the history of European progress, education generally lagged behind all through the nineteenth century; and even the reformers did not usually place America very high on the list of new subjects.

Thus, the introduction of American studies was bound to be gradual. It was dependent on the growth of the United States as a world power, and even more on the general progress in Europe of those liberal forces with which the United States had become associated. Advance was jerky, with great national differences, and preparations took time. The ninety years from the American Revolution to the American Civil War was a period of slow and sporadic beginnings.

The story opens with a fanfare. Never before or since has the United States carried such a message to the world as it did in the 1770's and 1780's. In a Europe constricted by dynasties and princes, by rigid class distinctions and ossified thoughts, enlightened philosophers had reveled in visions of a happier future. America demonstrated that "it could be done." From St. Petersburg to Lisbon, statesmen and writers studied the American experiment with a deep feeling of personal involvement; in the words of a Norwegian clergyman writing in 1781: "God help America to fight its way to liberty that mankind may not perish in serfdom." And when revolutionary fervor burst forth in France, America was there, symbolized in the memory of Benjamin Franklin, the idol of an entire generation of Europeans.

But decisive as this initial enthusiasm was to the future, in itself it was transitory. The great Revolution soon turned into something which the planners had not planned; and it was followed on its heels by violent reaction, against France and America alike. Empress Catherine II of Russia thought it piquant to hear about the exploits of the Americans; but when Alexander Radishchev began making unpleasant comparisons she promptly shipped him to Siberia. Moreover, these were turbulent times and little energy was left for educational reforms. This probably holds true without exception about secondary education, which is always a heavy machine to set into motion. Revolutionary France began a strong reform movement in her schools and also carried it into the nations she occupied. But this did not add to the popularity of the new ideas. Soon the regime was overthrown in France; and Napoleon at the height of his power had no love for America. Although no thorough investigation has been made of this subject as yet, there is no reason to believe that the United States was paid any real attention in European schools at this time.

Much more might have been expected from organized scholarship. The breakthrough of real European research on America is due to the revolutionary generation. The bulk of the immense literature that appeared about the New World was of course irresponsible journalism, often written "in the style of mythological tales." But it was paralleled by serious research, a fact which is often baffling when we remember the permanent shortage of material and the countless obstacles to scholarly American studies. Much of this work was animated by a strong liberal sympathy with the new republic; and quite often it showed an effort to interpret American Civilization as an integrated whole, in the spirit of Montesquieu and Herder. But as yet such scholarly efforts had scant support in the universities. The modern idea of the university as the home of organized research had not yet originated. Most universities were still as old-fashioned and retrospective as were the schools. Little if any attention was paid to modern subjects where the United States could come in. Scholars in the American field were usually learned noblemen or free-lance writers, not university professors. If they had a milieu it was that of the *littérateurs,* not of the classroom.

This situation was typical in Great Britain. The gentlemanly college thought much of manly sports and Latin, but had a profound contempt for real learning, and certainly did not intend to study that breakaway colony in America in any serious way. The Scotsmen felt somewhat differently about it even then. Some of the great Americanists of the period like William Robertson and William Russell were Scots, but the work of these men had no academic standing. The picture is similar for France. Quite important French literature, particularly on American government and economic life, was produced in the 1780's and 1790's; but the dry and mechanical teaching in the universities or *académies* certainly had little to do with it.

The nations of Southern Europe were in the same situation. The Enlightenment in Italy was relatively strong, and sometimes penetrated the walls of the universities. The first chair of political economy in Europe was established at Naples in 1754, and there was some early study of English. But America was still far away from the real traditions of Italy; and enlightened attempts were soon submerged by reaction. The greatest Italian contribution of the period, the *Historical and Political Investigation of the United States* (1788) by Filippo Mazzei, friend of Franklin, Jefferson, and Tsar Alexander I of Russia, was a work of love by a roving gentleman and free spirit. The situation was no more favorable in Spain, in Portugal, and in Austria, where the liberal historian of America Friedrich Wilhelm von Taube had several of his books forbidden by the censorship of Emperor Joseph II.

Even in the small nations it was apparently too early for

this kind of work. The freedom-loving republics of Switzerland were particularly open to American influences; and there were some unusual academic contacts. In 1794, for instance, plans were presented to Thomas Jefferson for moving the whole Academy of Geneva to the United States as the nucleus of an American university. But no American studies developed from these soundings. The famous work of Pictet de Rochemont, "de Genève" (1795), in which the United States was carefully described as "the example of the best liberty" is the manifesto of a statesman, not of a professor. It is probable that more exhaustive research will add to this picture. Thus, in the small university of Åbo in Finland the famous traveler Pehr Kalm, as professor in the 1750's, "presided at the defence of at least six theses on American topics," most of them probably on natural history. But as yet, we know little of what exists of this kind.

The great exception was Germany. Many German states of the time suffered as badly as any from bigotry, narrow-mindedness, and despotic rule. But there was also a strong enlightened movement, particularly in the northern states, which had more liberal regimes and were closely tied to England. Here connections with America developed early, both commercially and intellectually. A number of German writers of the period admired America; and from the 1760's this interest created original research of amazing strength. It was supported by a highly developed publishing business, which not only brought out a flood of travel books and literary works on the United States but almost as many publications of a scholarly kind. Between 1777 and 1797 three learned German journals were exclusively devoted to American studies.

From its very beginning this activity had its center in the universities; and different from the situation in England and

France, many of the German seats of learning were imbued with the spirit of the Enlightenment and were concerned with the study of contemporary life. These studies had their focus in the so-called "Statistics" which developed at Göttingen and represented a hybrid of present-day history, geography, and political science. The methods applied were sometimes surprisingly modern, such as seminars on "Contemporary History Studied in the Newspapers." Here America came into the picture early; at Göttingen specialized courses on the subject were given at least as early as 1778 and frequently thereafter. Similar work was doubtless carried on at other universities, such as Halle and Leipzig.

A number of the German scholars who wrote books on America also taught in the universities, forming a real school of American studies. Some of these scholars were conservatives and harshly critical of the United States. Most of them were probably liberals, and they were as friendly to the new republic in their teaching as they dared to be. But typical of them was a standard of objectivity and a broad sweep that was implied in "Statistics" itself: they expected to embrace all of American culture. At the same time a certain dualism was apparent which was going to be of momentous import in German development: on one side there was a myopic worship of detail, noncommittal in the pejorative sense, and on the other, "a trend towards intuitive synthesis bordering on the mystical." But on the whole the contribution of these scholars is impressive, equally in its volume and its methods.

Leader of the school, although he did not teach at a university, was that colossus of learning Christoph Ebeling, who was as well versed in American literature as in American politics and agriculture, and who based his research on an immense correspondence and on an American book collection which is now one of the treasures of the Widener Library at

Harvard. He brought together his results in the seven volumes of a *North American Geography and History* (1793–1816) which covers ten of the states. The book is a kind of prototype of the "area studies" of later times, and Ebeling suffused it with his own love of the "Mother Country of Liberty" which he had never seen with his own eyes.

This flowering was followed by a cold spell which seemed to make the hopeful beginnings only an interlude. The Revolutionary and Napoleonic wars dropped an iron curtain between the United States and Europe. When the curtain lifted again, the prospects looked bleak indeed for any American influence. With few exceptions the countries of Europe were governed by the forces of political reaction, organized in the Holy Alliance and having in common an elaborate ideology which condemned anything the United States stood for. In 1824 Chateaubriand, as French Minister of Foreign Affairs, declared the political principles of America to be "directly at variance with those of every other power."

Cultural reaction was no less wholesale and organized, in religion as in literature, and saw little of value in frontier America. The flowering of contemporary British literature made the American offerings appear even less striking; in the words of T. S. Eliot, "It is only in retrospect that their Americanness is fully visible." American culture did not appear quite as fashionable, even to many Americans.

Soon, however, it became clear that this reaction was not going to last. In the 1820's liberalism reappeared, consciously built on the heritage of the Enlightenment, and in spite of countless setbacks it proved to represent the "wave of the future," even before the time of the Civil War. Here the American political heritage again became a power of international importance. The broadening of democracy in the United States worked both ways; among other things, it created an active American interest in the revolutionary movements in Europe, an attitude which was symbolized by Daniel Webster's gesture toward the Hungarians in 1848. These ties across the ocean were strengthened by the rising tide of immigration. The reports of the immigrants with their democratic optimism worked as a liberal impulse in Europe and added fresh color to the image of America as the "Utopia of the Common Man." Here there were many crosscurrents; even European liberals often felt hesitant toward the strange new world with its plutocracy and "mobocracy," its enigmas and confusions. But it was the positive image that grew in strength, and this fitted in with the beginning democratization and modernization of Europe itself.

In this development, education was not in the vanguard, however. On the contrary, in most of the countries of Europe, education still tried to stay away from all modern and dangerous subjects. Schools without Latin were regarded as hotbeds of "materialism, atheism, and revolutionary disobedience." In spite of such resistance, more recent subjects began to make some headway. But the classical school was still predominant, and its advocates looked with extreme suspicion on the transatlantic newcomer and his often curious behavior.

In a number of countries the resistance to American studies was still political. In many nations of Eastern Europe, such as Greece and Hungary, we have testimonies of strong American sympathies; the Czechs published a whole American *bibliotéka* of translations in the middle of the century. But in most of these countries, and particularly in Austria, the governments had good reasons not to emphasize such materials in education. This was even more the case in Russia.

The liberal teaching at Göttingen had influenced a number of young Russian noblemen who went to the German university for their studies. Among the "Decembrists" who were sentenced to death in 1825 for their revolutionary plans against the Tsar, at least four were well-known admirers of the United States. As a consequence, America became a forbidden country in Russian education for several decades; Nicholas I even found it necessary to ban the teaching in the universities of comparative constitutional law. This, however, did not prevent America from playing a part in Russian radical thinking, from Herzen and Bakunin to Kropotkin. When the reactionary wave subsided, American geography and history appeared specifically in the Russian secondary schools; there is even a curious report to the effect that in 1858 Alexander II made "the American language" a subject in the military academies. But a new wave of reaction soon put an end to such experiments.

The situation was not much different in Italy and Spain. There was a strong sympathetic interest in American democracy; Mazzini and Garibaldi regarded the United States as "the sole bulwark against European despotism." But the school system in both nations was still extremely old-fashioned and often subject to political pressure. There is a report to the effect that King Ferdinand II of Naples (popularly called King Bomba because he once bombed his own citizens) imprisoned a professor in 1858 for his friendly reference to George Washington in a lecture. The incident has not been verified, but it may well be authentic.

Thus it was the three leading Western powers who continued to represent the European mainstream before the Civil War, even in the field of American studies. But here again the same America, working on various national minds, brought out differences as well as similarities.

Great Britain in this period saw the first beginnings of its much-needed school reform. But this was an uphill job. Even in the nineteenth century the British public schools and colleges were largely absorbed in the past; as late as 1936, the famous public school of Eton had four teachers of history, thirty-six of the classics. For the rest, British education relied on what Talleyrand called "the Englishman's privilege of ignorance"; in addition, there was still much inner resistance to the United States.

This held true of American literature in particular. There was considerable public interest in American writing in Great Britain, particularly among critics who were "extreme liberals or radicals in politics or Scotsmen by birth, or both." There was a history of American literature with a Scottish imprint as early as 1856. Washington Irving was used for language exercises in British schools, as he was everywhere in Europe; in 1855 the boys at Harrow decided by a formal vote that Longfellow was the first poet of the age. But these Americans were read as "English" authors—anything else would have been regarded as ridiculous. Famous is Matthew Arnold's outburst at the sight of a primer of American literature: "Imagine the face of Philip or Alexander at hearing of a primer of Macedonian literature!"

Even other fields were not much better off. History as a subject was held in general contempt in British schools as a soft option, and the teaching which existed in spite of this was centered on classical and British history. Reference to America was almost exclusively limited to the Revolution, which, in the words of G. M. Trevelyan, "can hardly be made an agreeable story to Englishmen." Even so, requirements were not excessive. In a report about Eton in 1834 it was stated that a boy "may pass through the school without disgrace and fancy that America was discovered by one

Washington and that one Columbus effected a wicked and bloody revolution somewhere in those parts."

The universities did not go much further. They were intent on building a "round" gentleman, who could serve without disgrace in Parliament or in the Colonies. For neither purpose was a knowledge of America of much avail. It was frankly declared that the United States "had no history"; and the reputation of the subject was hardly enhanced by friendly dilettantes like Charles Kingsley or political firebrands like Goldwin Smith, who tried to introduce it into academic teaching. The most impressive scholarly contribution of the period in Great Britain probably was the American history (1836) written by a learned Scottish lawyer, James Grahame, who never held a university position and whose "thoroughly American spirit" prevented the success of his work in England.

Quite different was the picture presented by France. The period opened with anti-American propaganda, initiated by the Restoration and Louis XVIII, continued under Charles X, and revived by Napoleon III. But beneath this surface a strong liberal American tradition remained. The United States reappeared all the time in the polemics of the opposition. The trend was symbolized by the return of Lafayette to French politics in 1830 and by the general enthusiasm for America in 1848; throughout the period of Napoleon III republicanism had one of its secret sources beyond the Atlantic. And this political concern ran parallel with an intensive interest in American literature and civilization, symbolized in Alexis de Tocqueville's masterly work *Democracy in America* (1835–40), the most influential book on America ever written by a European.

In this relationship there were countless ups and downs, particularly in education, where one reform killed another in confusing sequence. But in the continuous oscillation, the United States and its culture once in a while appeared on the surface and usually were promoted by some liberal regime. The French schools were still largely devoted to endless exercises in oratory and Latin verse-making. The teaching of English remained an hors d'oeuvre of small importance. But recent history became the pet of the reformers, and America benefited from it. At the end of the period the regulations of 1863 required from the graduating French schoolboy knowledge of the American Revolution and the American Constitution, the reasons for the swift rise of the Union, the Gold Rush and its repercussions in Europe, and the Mexican and the Civil wars, with a considerable quantity of details.

Unfortunately such efforts had little backing from the universities. All through the period they remained badly staffed and equipped; in 1830 the Faculty of Letters in Paris had only twelve full professorships, and it still had the same number in 1874. Much of the teaching consisted of public lectures, which often abounded in superficial rhetoric. There were a few professors of foreign literature, but they mainly taught German.

The great exception was in history and constitutional law. From the 1840's at least, scholars of standing such as Jules Michelet and Edouard Laboulaye used their public lectures at the Sorbonne and the Collège de France for a liberal discussion of American history. But they did so at definite political risks, and the subject formed no established part of the work of the ordinary student. In 1843 "American History to the Death of Washington" was actually posed as one of the questions at the competitive examination of the *agrégation;* but the entire degree was temporarily suppressed soon thereafter by Napoleon III.

Thus it was Germany which again showed the most continuous progress. The story is in many ways a tragic one. The great promises of the German uprising against Napoleon were never fulfilled. Reaction was soon back in power; a victorious liberal tradition was never established in Germany. But the progressive forces were not totally quenched. They reappeared again and again, and often referred to an American heritage. There was a scholarly tradition to build on. There were some free republics in the North, and also some other regimes where modern ideas had room to breathe. The influence of liberal emigrants to the United States was particularly strong in Germany, from Franz Lieber to Carl Schurz. And from the middle of the century public interest in America again took on surprising proportions as witnessed by German series of American literary texts, original and translated, which ran into hundreds of volumes.

This impact left its mark even on the schools. While the German classical *Gymnasium* had much more of an intellectual horizon than had the grammar schools of contemporary England or France, it was almost as negative when it came to the recent past, and English was usually not taught at all except on a voluntary basis. But in the *Realschools,* which sprang up in the 1840's under the impact of the new pedagogy, English was obligatory, and here an early interest developed in American literature. In 1854 the well-known educator L. Herrig brought out for the *Realschools* a work which had no parallel elsewhere in contemporary Europe, a handbook of the American classical authors, with 430 pages of text and with an American literary history of 120 pages, written in protest against British prejudices. The book was probably used very little—it was never reprinted. But afterwards Herrig included a large American section in his general anthology of English literature, which dominated the German market into the twentieth century; and some of these American texts, at least, were probably read on occasion. Much more important was the development within the German universities. Early in the century they were reorganized in a way which was to serve as a model to the rest of Europe. From the very beginning they showed some of the weaknesses which have followed them to this day, above all a trend of isolation from society and its demands. But this trend was not general; some of the universities of the time could be called "the last bulwarks of German freedom." Here the tradition of American studies was revived.

Little was done in geography, which had not yet found its modern methods. Even the study of English remained weak, without any specialized chairs. A number of American literary histories appeared for the German general public from the early 1850's onward, and there was an early interest in the American language. But it was probably unusual when in 1847 a university *Lektor* read Washington Irving with the students and when between 1841 and 1860 another read for six terms on Irving and Longfellow.

The important thing was not American books but American life, as studied in history and its adjacent fields. The study of "Statistics" now began to disappear in favor of specialized work in history inspired by Ranke. But the strong political involvement remained, and also the undaunted interest in contemporary events. In the winter term of 1848-49 the University of Berlin offered a course on "The Origins and Beginnings of the Recent Revolutions."

America, too, was given considerable attention in these studies. During the fifty years from 1820 to 1870 German universities announced about two hundred and fifty courses in which America was specifically mentioned in the title, and about half of these were exclusively devoted to the United States. This amounts to about five courses a year as an average, a figure which is not too impressive when we remember that Germany had seventeen universities at the time. But it represents a definite effort, and doubtless was matched by similar attention in general courses. (We know that Ranke, for instance, always included America in his lectures on world history.) In some larger universities specific courses about America were almost annual; in Berlin there were usually two to three a year after the middle 1840's.

Of particular interest is the political character of this teaching. Some of it was neutral or conservative; but a number of the professors in question were fighting liberals who taught American studies in the service of their ideals. There was a significant rise in the number of American courses around 1830 and 1848, the years of revolution; and quite a few of the professors suffered political persecution for their views. This teaching was backed by a scholarship of surprising range and quality, both in and outside the universities. There was even an early academic interest in the story of the American impact. In 1843 Professor F. W. Schubert in Königsberg gave a course entitled "The Influence of the United States, East India, and China on Europe."

The importance of this work should not be exaggerated. The number of American courses was still small, and they were rarely made part of any established program. But taken together they mean something; and they became influential even outside Germany, in the nations which more or less had adopted the German system of education. In the Netherlands with their dominant classical tradition and their limited emigration to America little was done as yet, apart from a few doctoral theses. But in Norway between 1850 and 1859 the leading conservative statesman, A. M. Schweigaard taught four specialized courses at Christiania (Oslo) on United States statistics (in the modern economic sense), and a little later there were similar courses at Uppsala in Sweden. In Copenhagen, Denmark, three term courses were devoted to Longfellow in 1857–58.

Most important was the follow-up in Switzerland, which received its impulse from both Germany and France. In French-speaking Geneva the liberal statesman James Fazy, "the creator of modern Geneva," who was reared on American ideals by Lafayette himself, came to power in 1846 and governed the city as a people's tribune for a quarter of a century. In 1848 the English language was made optional in the classical college of the city. The Academy of Geneva was modernized; and in 1852 Fazy called from Paris as professor of law the republican Alexandre Laya, author of a work on the institutions of France and America. He began his activity at Geneva by courses in 1852–54 on "The Laws, Institutions, and Economic Movement of England and America and their Influence on the Monarchic or Republican States in the Nineteenth Century." In the German-speaking parts of Switzerland quite extensive teaching on the civilization of the United States began in the 1830's at the reorganized universities, in American history and particularly in American constitutional law. Much of this teaching had a strong liberal character, and in the early decades was sometimes not void of danger. A number of the scholars in the field were political refugees from Germany.

As this material clearly shows, these were the times of origin and preparation. There was still no defined discipline of American studies. There was no single chair in any American subject. The United States had hardly any established place in curricula and requirements. But there was something that is even more important—a keen feeling in the best minds that America was of relevance and had to be worked into the system of organized knowledge. The spirit of this initial period may be caught most appropriately in a few biographical glimpses of men who carried the brunt of pioneering.

Among the early generation was the German historian Johan Kortüm, born in 1788 and reared in liberal Göttingen as a fervent republican who saw his ideals realized in Greece, Rome, Switzerland, and the United States. His hatred of Napoleon made him set out as a volunteer for Spain; but he was captured and barely escaped death. Instead, he fought as a volunteer in the war from 1813 to 1814 and reveled in the Paris libraries as a soldier of occupation. He spent his middle years as a migrant scholar in Austria and Switzerland, and in Basel and Bern in the 1820's and 1830's taught American history and the history of republicanism, receiving much praise for his brusque honesty and undaunted speech. He published in Zürich his history of the North American revolution (1829) before he moved on to liberal Heidelberg, to continue and conclude his work in his homeland.

To a later generation belonged the Briton Goldwin Smith, born in 1823. He was a man with a most solid classical education, who turned into a politician and radical, a journalist and pamphleteer, a sponsor of unpopular causes, the horror of respectable Oxford dons; in the *Dictionary of National Biography* his profession is given as "controversialist." He was a follower of Cobden and Bright, an advocate of the emancipation of the British colonies, and during the American Civil War an agitator for the Union cause. His writings are the works of a moralist "not too interested in historical sources," his study of the foundation of the American colonies largely a document of his own democratic ardor. When in 1858 he was appointed professor of modern history at Oxford he pleaded in his inaugural address for the widening of the old curricula, and he also occasionally lectured thereafter on American history. But his missionary zeal made little impression. In 1866 he moved across the ocean to Cornell, and later went to live in Toronto, writing his American history there and fighting for all his good causes. He did not die until 1910. Finally, there was Edouard Laboulaye, born in 1811, reared in the French liberal tradition. His life was that of a citizen, a *vulgarisateur* of the first order, journalist, pamphleteer, novelist, parliamentarian, orator. He was the author of one of the most devastating attacks ever to appear against Napoleon III. At the same time he was a scholar with an impressive production in political science and the history of law; and in all these fields his thoughts and actions were permeated by his admiration for the United States. As a professor at the Collège de France he lectured in 1849 and again in 1861 on the political history of the United States; the lectures appeared in print in the 1850's and 1860's and were widely translated. He wrote on slavery in America, on Franklin, on the relationship of the United States and France; his most popular work was the semi-fictional *Paris en Amérique*. But all his activity served the great Franco-American tradition; and he lived to see the Emperor overthrown and the Third Republic based on the ideals of that heritage.

These are motley careers. By our standards of scholarship one might have several things to say about them. But these men sensed the dawn of greater things to come.

2. New Enigmas for Old (1865–1918)

WHEN, on April 26, 1865, the London *Daily News* carried a report in its second edition about the assassination of President Lincoln, the impression on the British metropolis was immense. Four shillings each were paid for copies of the paper. The sensation was no less staggering elsewhere. Not since the murder of Henry IV of France had Europe rung with such excitement.

There was of course a strong feeling of the human and personal tragedy involved in these sentiments. But perhaps the shock also mingled with some realization of the momentous importance of that conflict which had now come to its dramatic close. As a matter of fact, the Civil War was to give the United States a completely new position in the world. And the change was to be much more ambiguous than Lincoln's mourners could possibly realize on that April afternoon.

Within the framework settled by the war, the American nation saw a general expansion which has few equals in modern history. The territory of the republic increased and its population soared. Its economic and industrial growth was explosive; almost overnight its display of strength gave the United States a voice in world politics. In its cultural life the nation showed a frontier buoyancy which lustily applied the techniques of the machine age; and the international sales success of its products compensated for the lifted eyebrows of European connoisseurs. The two hemispheres were even brought closer to each other physically by the continued expansion of the steamship lines. Whatever might be the attitudes toward the United States in Europe, to overlook it was no longer possible.

This new America, which thus arose behind the morning fogs, in many ways was bound to scare the Old World. It called back to life many inveterate hesitations and added a few new ones.

Before the Civil War the United States had still been predominantly rural. The magnitude of the westward movement and typical life along the frontier were strange to European eyes. But the civilization which developed largely appeared as recognizable; somehow the inherited set of Old World standards could still be applied.

After the Civil War this was no longer true to the same extent. The new form of life which developed in America was characterized by a speed and dimension, a violence and recklessness which had no exact correspondence even in industrialized Europe. These qualities represented the beginnings of a development which in the future would be labeled as "typically American"; and to the cultivated European this new Americanism had a touch of the fantastic and terrifying. If the sympathy of most European conservatives was with the Confederacy, it was because they felt that somehow the South was the last representative of an American culture with which they could still identify themselves; and they were not altogether wrong.

American democracy after the great conflict showed many new and seamy sides. The hanging of the Haymarket anarchists shocked the world not much less than did the Sacco-Vanzetti case forty years later. Socialism became a power in Europe as a response to problems to which the American Way offered no solution; and Marxist ideas also reflected upon the image of the United States. American cultural life raised the problems of mass civilization, of its standards and values; and the beginning invasion of Europe by American travelers and American consumer goods brought the problems home. In 1901 the famous British journalist William T. Stead could write his book on *The Americanization of the World*. In the following year one of his French colleagues, using the same headline, prophesied that the American conqueror would "subjugate our spirit, change our mores and institutions, and overthrow the equilibrium of the civilized world."

These doubts, and many others, were going to play a decisive part in the reaction against the United States which was typical of the period after 1920. But as yet they were only in their beginnings. They had little strength except in certain nations or in certain layers of population; and they were counteracted by much stronger trends.

Apart from the more exotic features of American life, Europe's own development increasingly ran parallel with that of the United States. Political democracy followed its course on both sides of the ocean, and, as before, there was a keen feeling of fellowship and common interest. The growth of industrial capitalism was largely the same in America and Europe. The breakup of social stratification raised similar problems and sometimes created new fellowships. Intellectual and literary life in Europe more and more turned away from an idealistic philosophy to modernism, realism, positivism, and a practical pragmatism, as it did in the United States.

On all these points America was bound to appear less strange to young Europeans than it did to their fathers. The main trend was one of increasing closeness and positive interest. The hesitations were overshadowed by the immediate relevance of modern America to modern Europe; to William

T. Stead the Americanization of the world was largely a process to be welcomed. In the best minds, moreover, there was a dawning realization that "America" was no longer just America, but the spearhead of a general development, and that even the modern United States could only be understood in a global perspective and in the light of universal cultural problems.

All this meant that the need to know the United States, not only by hearsay but by systematic study and research, increased immensely throughout Europe after the American Civil War. As before, the development was jerky. But the movement itself was general, and the growth within European education now made it possible for this interest to become a force.

Even in European classrooms and lecture rooms, modern ism and realism gradually gained the upper hand. The shift was closely tied to the widening of the geographical horizon: a Europe absorbed in colonial policies and international competition could no longer believe in its own all-importance. The change was symbolized by a continued strengthening everywhere of the new *Realschools,* the educational instrument of the bourgeois class; by the declining importance of Greek and Latin in the curricula; and by the ascendency of modern history and modern languages—above all of English. In several countries this battle was decided in the favor of the modern subjects during the decades immediately following the American Civil War.

The universities showed a similar trend. Following the German lead, they were now everywhere being organized for research. Centers of this development were the new "institutes," in the European sense of the word—that is, research institutions with permanent libraries and staffs. From the 1890's on, the growth of modern studies in the traditional humanities was paralleled by the rise of new disciplines or by new expansion within old ones, such as comparative law, economics, and political and social sciences. This entire trend was bound to serve the development of American studies; from the 1890's on they were also furthered by the impact of American pedagogical reform. Moreover, as far as government regulation was concerned, the growing political might of America began to make itself directly felt in education. In several countries the relationship to the United States became an important factor in their foreign policies, with repercussions even in the cultural field.

Such facts should not leave the reader with the impression that in this period there was anything like a victorious movement of American studies. Many retarding forces were still powerful, even in education. General ignorance about America often remained shocking. The motives for change were less simple than before, and the contrasts within modern American life often made the study of it a subject hard to handle. In the over-all picture American work remained small. But the scattered efforts were much more numerous now than they had been before the Civil War. Sometimes they were organized into a planned advance toward a defined goal. And much more than before these American studies now came to be built on observation. From around 1900 outstanding European scholars began their exodus to the United States in preparation for their own teaching, a movement which has continued ever since.

Among the great Western Nations the United Kingdom even now held a place in the rear as far as American studies were concerned.

The general American influence in Great Britain rose

steeply following the Civil War. The outcome of the conflict added new strength to the British movements for democratization, politically and socially, and such transatlantic contacts continued; British labor leaders read Henry George and Edward Bellamy more keenly than they studied Karl Marx. The interrelations gradually touched upon almost all fields of life; for the sixteen years following 1898 this penetration has been described by Richard H. Heindel (1940) in the most intensive and comprehensive study to be made so far of the impact of America on one nation in one limited period. Toward the end of the century, foreign policy added a further incentive: Great Britain needed American support against the growing might of Germany. But in education it was still different. Progress of American studies was still halting; and the lack of centralization which is typical of the British educational system made everything depend on individual initiative.

In the British secondary schools there was still little more progress than there had been before. Even English history still struggled to gain any kind of recognition. As late as 1864 the Clarendon Educational Report stated that history "can never occupy a large space in a great classical school." Forty years later, in 1908, the British Board of Education in its recommendations did not mention American history for any of the forms except to include George Washington as an appropriate hero for boys under twelve.

American literature suffered the same fate. The first time the subject is mentioned by the British Board of Education is apparently in a report dating from 1921, and then only in order to explain why the United States had been unable to develop a national literature: "Its origins are too recent and the occupations of its people too modern."

In the universities the beginnings were not much more

promising. Typical of the general attitude is the famous incident in 1866 when a young and radical Liverpool merchant,
Henry Yates Thompson, offered to endow the University of
Cambridge with a readership for an American citizen in the
history, literature, and institutions of the United States, the
incumbent to be appointed by Harvard College. The offer
was not well received; in vain Professor Charles Kingsley
assured his colleagues that Harvard could be relied upon
not to stand for revolutionary principles. The Cambridge
University Senate rejected the offer by a vote of 107 to 81,
and even refused the use of one of the lecture halls for a single
course by way of experiment. Mentioned as reasons for the
denial were a general dislike of democracy, an unwillingness
to have the reader appointed by Unitarian Harvard, and "the
American self-conceit" that needed no further support.

But exactly at this time general reforms were under way.
The study of history was reorganized at Oxford and Cambridge under the leadership of W. Stubbs and J. R. Seeley.
Some of the teachers, among them Lord Acton, encouraged
work in American history, and specialized courses began to
appear. King's College in London, in 1864–65, announced
a course on American history to 1815, and at the same time
set a prize essay comparing *ingenium et mores* in the old
Athenians and in present-day Americans, a flattering juxta-
position. From the 1870's on, courses in American subjects
began to occur even at Oxford, Cambridge, and Edinburgh,
and from 1900 they became quite numerous, particularly in
geography and history.

But these historical studies largely remained limited to
the earlier periods. As late as 1914 the teaching of English
history at Oxford stopped at 1837. What was admitted of
American history was closely tied to that of the British Empire—it was the period of Joseph Chamberlain. And con-

nection with American scholarship was still weak. On the eve of the First World War some American historians were invited to teach at Oxford, and the Rhodes Scholarships opened new possibilities for exchange. But these were still straws in a not-too-strong wind.

A much less conventional approach was typical of the London School of Economics, which was founded in 1895. From its very beginning this school emphasized the study of day-to-day American developments; it was soon to be one of the great centers of American studies in Europe. But its radicalism still left the school without much of an influence in the old universities.

The same limitations appeared in research. Important work was done in Great Britain, particularly in American history and institutions, from W. Lecky to G. O. Trevelyan; but with the great exception of James Bryce, emphasis was strongly British. When in 1903 the American volume of the *Cambridge Modern History* appeared, it contained no contribution by an Englishman for the period after 1783 except on naval history.

Even more typical of the general attitude was the almost complete neglect of American intellectual and literary life. There was no lack of public interest—even Walt Whitman and Joaquin Miller found their literary advocates in England, and the University of Oxford in 1907 conferred its honorary doctorate upon Mark Twain, to his immense satisfaction. But this generosity had little to do with regular work within the university walls.

The entire study of literature had a strenuous birth at British universities; the new English departments were soon conquered by the German school of linguistics, which regarded historical grammar as the center of the world. Oxford had its first professor of English literature in 1885 after heated debates; the first incumbent of the chair, A. S. Napier, was a philologist who never in his lectures got beyond the Norman Conquest. (When once toward the end of his career Mr. Napier announced a course on Chaucer one of his colleagues teasingly expressed his surprise at this recognition of the "decadents.") When Cambridge had a similar chair of literature in 1910, it was declared by its opponents that such a professorship would be "of a light and comic character, not only useless but positively harmful." Modern British literature hardly had any place in this system, let alone the literature of America, a poor country that had not even a language of its own.

The outstanding exception in this generation of scholars was again a liberal and a Scot, John Nichol, a professor at the University of Glasgow who was attached to the United States both by his family, his travels, and his political radicalism. In 1882 Mr. Nichol brought out a bulky history of American literature, one of the few works of its kind ever to be produced by a British university scholar, based on lectures given in the 1860's and 1870's. But this activity certainly had nothing to do with ordinary teaching and requirements. When the *Cambridge History of English Literature* was planned (it first appeared in 1907) American literature was left to be handled by the Americans themselves, an ambiguous and revealing decision.

A totally different picture was presented by the two other great Western powers. In the decade following the American Civil War both France and Germany went through a similar ordeal, the Franco-German War in 1870–71; and the conflict was to influence both of them deeply, but in different ways.

In France the defeat made painfully obvious how little the country was up to its task in the modern world of technology and mass armies. A scathing criticism was directed against the governing classes, and quite particularly against the school system with its "piously guarded traditions from the Middle Ages." The reformers called for a general secularization and modernization based on the new spirit of civic responsibility. In the 1880's and 1890's, both schools and universities in France were gradually reorganized and subjected to a strict centralization. The schools were streamlined to serve "the multi-fold aspirations of modern life." In the universities the local *licence*, and above all the nationwide *agrégation,* were turned into formidable tests of tightly organized knowledge.

These reforms were based largely on models borrowed from the victorious Germans. But besides, there was a growing concern with the Anglo-Saxon nations. "What is the reason for their superiority?" asked a much discussed French book, and the Anglo-Saxon educational systems were mentioned in explanation. This curiosity continued to grow in strength. More and more Frenchmen realized that the United States after the Civil War was going through a tremendous development to which France had not paid sufficient attention. "We have long enough taken the Greeks and Romans as our models," one of the radical educators wrote in 1885. "Let us try to study the English and the Americans and open our eyes at last to the light of the modern world."

Such ideas also had a political background. French authoritarianism again raised its head after 1871, and it was only after some time that the Third Republic was established on democratic foundations; here American ideals reappeared as part of the revolutionary tradition. And there were even more urgent demands. France in the 1890's was under political pressure both from Great Britain and Germany; it well needed to emphasize its American relations.

This movement toward American studies was apparent from the very end of the Franco-German war. Important was an institution outside the university tradition, the Ecole Libre des Sciences Politiques in Paris. This school was founded in 1871 out of the very defeat, in an effort to give scholarship a new place in society. (The institution was to serve in the 1890's as a model for the London School of Economics and in the 1920's for a similar institution in Berlin.) From its very foundation, the Ecole Libre paid regular attention to contemporary America, both in teaching and research; and similar work, sometimes with an outspoken liberal note, appeared spontaneously in several universities long before the reorganization.

But decisive to the whole movement was the interest shown in the subject by the French educational authorities with their strongly centralized power. Parallel to the great reforms in school and university, the French Ministry of Public Instruction from the 1880's on adopted a policy of giving more attention in both teaching and examinations to the United States and its civilization. The reform does not seem to have caused much discussion. It was rather regarded as a matter of course: America just was there, and it had to be noticed.

These efforts were apparent even in the secondary schools; but the most important work was done in the universities. And for the first time this activity was supported by organized academic exchange. Since 1871 Germany had become the Mecca of American scholars and students who traveled abroad—very few of them went to France any more. Toward the end of the century serious efforts were made to renew the connections, by sizable grants both from French and American sources. It was under such arrangements, for instance, that Charles Cestre and André Siegfried went to the United States in the late 1890's and that scholars such as Barrett Wendell, George Santayana, and Bliss Perry lectured at the Sorbonne from 1904 on. A purely American contribution was the establishment in 1895 of the Franklin Library in Paris.

In some branches of learning, particularly in law, and in the political and social sciences, these new American studies were largely limited to work for the doctorate. But in subjects such as geography and history, with their central place in the schools, the added importance of American material was obvious on all levels of study. From the 1880's down to the First World War, questions in American geography and history appeared on the program of the rigorous examination for the *agrégation* at least every third year, probably even more frequently. The same was apparently the case at the *licence* in a number of universities. And in accordance with the French system, where teaching closely corresponded to the programs, American geography and history thus automatically began to play a considerable part in academic lecturing from the 1880's on. Quite often these courses were given by first-rate scholars such as Georges Weill, Henri Hauser, Albert Mathiez, and Emile Bourgeois. In the great French world history, similar to the *Cambridge Modern History,* which was published by Lavisse and Rambaud in 1901, there was no difficulty in having the American section covered by a French scholar.

Even more impressive was the development with regard to American literature. From the 1880's on, English was gradually introduced at the French universities as a separate subject; and these studies were not suffocated by an exaggerated emphasis on Anglo-Saxon, as was the case in England and Germany, but had their focus in the famous French *explication*, a literary method which combines a close reading of the text with a keen interest in the civilization from which it originates. French research in modern British literature soon came to surpass that of every other foreign nation; and American literature was included in this activity as well. The interest was also reflected outside the universities in a new school of literary critics of American writing. But what distinguished these studies in France was their recognition as a normal part of the academic system, in a way which had no parallel elsewhere at the time.

The beginning was made in the *agrégation*, the nationwide competitive test which qualifies the successful candidate for the highest paid teaching positions in school. The annual program for this examination in English at the time listed twelve authors for compulsory study. From the early 1880's on, one or two American literary works were included in this list almost every second year on an average; and they had to be studied with the severity demanded in an examination where normally 90 per cent of the candidates are flunked. There was a similar inclusion among the compulsory texts in several of the lower nation-wide examinations, and at the *licence;* sometimes the subjects were extraordinary, such as "Emerson as a Pessimist" and "The Humor of Edgar Allan Poe."

These requirements were followed up by ordinary courses of American literature that were pioneering in character. In 1868 a German-born professor at Caen gave a general survey course on the subject, "a young literature about which our old Europe hardly has any idea"; apparently it was the first course of its kind to be announced in a European university. From the 1880's American teaching became regular in connection with the new programs; the first general survey course of this kind, comprising thirteen American authors from Franklin to Longfellow and Motley, was apparently given at Poitiers in 1888, at a time when such courses were almost nonexistent in American colleges.

Even academic research got under way. From 1887 to the First World War the University of Paris alone accepted an average of one doctoral thesis a year on American subjects, and there were also some dissertations in the universities in the provinces. Many of these theses moved within the domain of American politics, economy, and law; but there were also some French *thèses d'état* on American literature, formidable both in quantity and quality.

These efforts still had to struggle against much resistance, and sometimes of a quite primitive kind. As late as 1909 there was a great discussion in a French educational journal on the advisability of students of English visiting the United States. It was maintained that America was so different from France as to make an American experience of dubious value; and the students were warned against the dangerous "state of flux" in the American language: one does not go to Switzerland or Belgium for the study of French, "and the Swiss and Belgians speak that language much better than the Americans speak English!" It has to be added that these warnings were sounded by Britons, writing to the editor; but doubtless they had the sympathy of many Frenchmen as well.

There was a resistance deeper down. In spite of its surface revolutions, France did not go through as thorough an economic and social transformation in the nineteenth century as that which was typical of contemporary England and Germany. French small-bourgeois conservatism remained unperturbed, and it was to reassert itself again and again, even in French relations with America.

But taken as a whole, France in the period in question reaffirmed its allegiance to the great Western traditions which had played such a decisive part in its history. The new interest in America and its civilization fits into this pattern. The organized French efforts in American studies between the Civil and the First World War represent one of the first serious steps taken in the field by a European government. The future development in France was to move within the framework established before 1900.

A movement similar in result but deeply different in character took place at the same time in Germany.

To the Germans, the victory in the war of 1870–71 meant a tremendous national experience. After generations of particularism and political flux, the establishment of the German Empire gave the nation a feeling of powerful optimism, of unity and purpose. The war was followed by a growth of industry and of cities which in many ways paralleled that of post-bellum America and brought the nations more closely together. The new German business class demanded a strengthening of transatlantic ties. The new German mass emigration to the United States in the 1880's and 1890's created new and friendly contacts. German intellectual life became cosmopolitan; by 1900 an observer could call Hamburg and Berlin the most Americanized cities of Europe. And in both the urban and rural populations, interest in America was growing throughout the period; seventeen German travel books on the United States appeared between 1903 and 1906 alone. And this whole development took place within the framework of a parliamentary democracy, established and functioning with German efficiency, where the liberal leaders looked to the West for their ideological support as the previous generation of German liberals had done under the autocratic princes.

This interest in the United States was gradually shared by the German authorities as well. Bismarck had many American ties from his early youth on; Carl Schurz in 1868 found Bismarck better informed on American conditions than any European he had met. As Chancellor of the new Empire, Bismarck saw the cultivation of German-American relations as a part of his foreign policy, and in that respect at least he was followed by Wilhelm II. From 1905 on, the so-called "Theodore Roosevelt Professorships" made it possible to have a number of American scholars teach American Civilization at German universities. For the purpose of wider cultural contacts, an independent American Institute with a large library was opened in 1910 in Berlin. And parallel with these efforts, from the very establishment of the Empire, steps were taken both on higher and lower levels to give the United States more attention in German education. It seemed that after its many years of tribulation Germany had now finally made up its mind to base its development on the common heritage of the democratic West.

As in France, the secondary schools with their great local differences lagged considerably behind. The requirements in American history were strengthened and more American authors were probably read in class, but not many. In a Prussian survey in 1897, Washington Irving occupied the sixth place on the English reading list, Frances Hodgson Burnett was number eighteen, Franklin number twenty-two, and Longfellow number twenty-five. It was the universities which really had something to show.

During this period the German universities went through a flowering that has never been equaled since. They enjoyed generous government support, their recruitment of talent was impressive, and their organization splendid. Contrary to the French system, their regulations were usually vague. Everything depended on the individual teacher, above all on the full professor, who held "the most independent position in which a German can be placed"; and his purpose was to educate the students, not for a profession, but for scholarship. What the German professor included in his teaching largely determined the place of any subject, as clearly as did the state regulations in France and the set papers in Great Britain. Here the United States and its civilization now made a great stride forward.

In geography, specialized courses on the United States became practically regular. Between 1870 and 1880 no more than a third of German universities announced such courses; between 1910 and 1918 there were only two which did not. American history made similar progress from the 1890's on; in the four largest universities, specialized courses on the subject were given every year or every two years, and further specialization was always possible. The first professorship of American studies to be established at any European university was that of "American Political and Constitutional History," which was in existence for a few years in the early 1870's at the German University of Strasbourg.

More important than this framework was the number of young scholars, above all young historians, who now went into the American field and supplemented their research in secondary sources with studies on the spot; among them were three of the leading scholars of the period, Herman Oncken, Erich Marcks, and Karl Lamprecht. And these students of America were involved in scholarly debates on the highest level. Against the political historians with their specialized and narrow nationalism, Lamprecht raised the idea of a synthetic and speculative world history concerned with mass movements and the morphology of cultures. In his program of scholarly integration even the United States played its part; in the Institute for the History of World Civilization which Lamprecht founded at Leipzig, America was to have its obvious place.

There was a surprising awareness of all aspects of American life, from politics and economics to education and religion. The theologian Karl Bornhausen in 1912 founded a Theological America-Library at Marburg for the purpose of studying American theology and religion as parts of the entire social, economic, and intellectual life of the United States.

American literature, on the contrary, worked against severe handicaps. English philology, which the Germans developed from the 1870's on, and which was soon imitated throughout the world, was almost exclusively focused on the older periods of language, while modern literature and the spoken tongue were regarded with outright suspicion. From the 1880's however, a countermovement arose, advocating a *Kulturkunde* which emphasized the homogeneous character of all national civilizations, even in our own time, and the importance of studying them in all their aspects. Here American literature gradually gained some ground. The first general survey courses were given in 1887 and following years, almost exactly at the time when similar courses were first given in France. After 1900 such courses grew in number and were sometimes given by scholars of the first rank. Even doctoral theses became more common. Of course, they were still relatively few; during the twenty years preceding the end of the First World War German universities accepted nineteen theses on American literature, but eighty-two on Shakespeare. Compared with the previous decade, however, progress was considerable; and it was matched by independent research. Since 1900 and down to this day, an average of one German book on American literature has appeared annually, not including doctoral dissertations.

These were encouraging signs. But seen in retrospect, the shortcomings appear as no less momentous.

The Germany of the Empire seemed to have broken with its authoritarian past. But the nation was not yet prepared for self-government. Many traditional strongholds of power remained, from the landed aristocracy to the military caste; and in their reactionary and chauvinist policies they were often supported by the new capitalist class. In such circles, with their great political influence, the democratic United States was detested. At the same time, America with its strong German population played a part in queer imperialistic hopes and fancies, which were supported by the apparent meeting of minds between Wilhelm II and President Theodore Roosevelt.

German universities on the whole were allied with these conservative and nationalist powers. German scholarship reflected only a part of the life of the nation, even in its relation to America; and the new American studies offered no real counterpoise. On the contrary, some of the leading academic students of the United States visualized an America which did not exist, an America dominated by its German immigrants, which eventually would break away from its pacifist and democratic past and join Germany in the conquest of the world. In August, 1914, Karl Lamprecht could encourage his fellow countrymen marching off to the battlefields by pointing to an America tied to Germany by the bonds of "Teutonism" against "semi-Celtic" and decadent Britain. Such pipe dreams were sadly misleading with regard to the coming war. They were even more ominous for German development after the war.

This gradual progress of American studies was duplicated in several of the other European nations. In Austria the University of Vienna as early as 1862 offered a course on "The Physical, Technical, and Intellectual Growth of North America, Compared to that of the Western European States," and from the 1880's on, American courses of many kinds became relatively frequent at Austrian and Czech universities. In the German-speaking parts of Switzerland the development often followed the German timetable, and the French-speaking parts paralleled the movement in France, only more sporadically. Thus, in the 1870's, the tiny University of Neuchâtel established as part of its *licence* in English a program of American literary studies which would appear impressive even today, only to drop it again in the 1880's. There were also notable efforts in Scandinavia.

But this bright picture had somber shadows. The negative aspects, which still lurked beneath the surface in Germany, came out into the open in the south and east of Europe.

Unified and liberated Italy might seem to have many reasons for cultivating its ties with the United States. Italian liberalism had an old American background. Italian mass emigration from the 1880's made the United States familiar to the entire population and created much general good will.

But democracy and its traditions remained a foreign importation in Italy. Even much more than in Germany, Italy's political life was dominated by the aristocratic traditions of the past; there was little soil for the liberal heritage of the West. Italian parliamentarism proved powerless in the face of the problems of Italian poverty. And the Catholic Church remained a solid block in the road of progressive thought. The special heresy of "Americanism" was explicitly condemned by the pope in 1899.

Italian education remained an equally closed system, weighted down by an excessive classical nationalism. Of the weekly hours in the *ginnasio,* more than 75 per cent were originally dedicated to Greek, Latin, and Italian; and many successive reforms did not break this pattern. England had hardly any place on the syllabus, and America, of course, even less. A "modern" *ginnasio* was introduced in 1910, with English and American compulsory requirements, but the school was abolished after a few years. In the universities, there was considerable independent research in fields like American education and philosophy, history and politics, and often with a liberal tendency. But the system of teaching and examinations was hopelessly retrospective, and out of touch with present-day realities.

Behind this aloofness there was a general reserve. It was expressed in intellectual terms in the books of the famous historian Guglielmo Ferrero, where he contrasted the "quantitative" trend of modern America with the alleged clarity and balance of the "Latin mind." But there was also a conscious political reaction, expressed in the early pre-fascist movements. Their mouthpiece, the poet Gabriele d'Annunzio, could on occasion enlist for his purpose the image of a Whitmanesque American superman. But at bottom, this school of thought took its stand against all that represents America's real tradition, and cultivated ideas that were fraught with dangers for the future.

A similar situation prevailed in Spain. Spanish liberals remained strongly interested in American federal democracy. In the revolutionary decade around 1870, French and American republicanism had a joint impact on Spanish thought, and some efforts were made to introduce English in the schools. Similarly, the young "generation of '98" tried to cultivate American contacts as part of the bitterly needed "Westernization" of Spain. But even more than in Italy the strength of the past was overwhelming. To Spanish intellectuals the Anglo-Saxon nations still seemed to exist at a tremendous distance; among 40,000 volumes ordered for use in the University Library of Madrid in the year 1893–94, no more than 152 volumes were in English. And in the background the authoritarian tradition remained. After each foray into liberalism, power was apt to return to its traditional wielders: the landlords, the Church, and the Crown, with their aversion to anything which America traditionally stands for.

The other extreme in this precarious balance appeared at the other end of Europe, in Russia.

The new wave of political oppression from the 1880's on rather served to strengthen Russian liberalism with its old strand of American thought. Some of the leading Russian students of America in the period were exiles. But those liberals who remained at home made the universities into the "chief centers of revolt"; when the tables were turned in 1905 these liberals undertook the heavy task of making tsarist Russia into a parliamentary democracy.

But there was another school of Russian thinkers on America. They had gradually turned away from the reformist ideology, and found their guidance in Karl Marx. Some of them still looked hopefully to the United States; but others increasingly came to regard America as the great negative example, no more from a conservative but from a radical point of view. Before the First World War this group was still in the background; but the future was with them. After 1917, they were to give their note to Russian development and to turn their anti-Americanism into a world force.

If this story is again summed up by a few biographical sketches, the picture still has its trend of political oppression and of bitter struggles, as it had in the period of the Holy Alliance. But as a whole, the situation was brightening. American studies were gaining in academic respectability. In most nations they were carried on the victorious wave of political liberalism; and this change was reflected in the fates of the individuals.

Hermann von Holst still belonged to the "old" generation. He was born in the Baltic parts of Russia; he was active as a revolutionary, barely escaped Siberia, and in 1867 arrived in the United States, so poor that he had to stay in bed on the days when his single shirt was laundered. These conditions did not prevent him from publishing in the following year his *Pen Drawings from the History of Absolutism.* After earning his spurs as a journalist he was asked by merchants in Bremen to settle in Germany and to take up American studies in the interest of German-American relations. He was appointed in 1872 to the new American chair at Strasbourg, and two years later moved to Freiburg, where he wrote his monumental four-volume *Constitutional History of the United States* (1878–91). He returned to America in 1892 and for his twelve remaining years used his extraordinary oratory and his political insight in the fight against American imperialism —a liberal in the grand style, fostered equally by Europe and America, he was honored equally by both.

On a more modest scale, there is the same note of success about J. J. Rüttimann. He was one of the leading reformers of mid-century Switzerland, and active in many fields of Swiss public life; his name is connected with economic reforms as well as with the reorganization of criminal, civil, and military law. But his whole thinking was penetrated by

American political ideas (although he never went to the United States). As early as in 1848 he had the American two-chamber system of government introduced in Switzerland. As a law professor in Zürich he taught the American Constitution as one of his favorite subjects; and his main scholarly work was a broad and authoritative comparison of American and Swiss constitutional life (1867–76), simultaneous with that of Hermann von Holst and with a similar brilliance of learning.

In Great Britain James Bryce moved on the same level: Professor of Civil Law at Oxford from 1870 onwards, famous specialist on the Holy Roman Empire, traveler and mountaineer, orator and politician, Cabinet member, and Chief Secretary for Ireland, celebrated as educator and statesman on the national and international scale. Among all these activities he wrote, almost as a recreation, his *American Commonwealth* (1888), a work based on unbreakable faith in democratic principles, which remains a classic to this day. He used six of his last years to cement Anglo-American friendship as British Ambassador to Washington.

There is a touch of final triumph even in the life story of the Russian Moisey Yakovlevich Ostrogorsky. Like Hermann von Holst he left his country because of his political opinions; he studied America at the Paris Ecole Libre des Sciences Politiques and gathered his results in his famous work, written in French, on the *American Political Parties* (1902). He was filled by a deeper skepticism toward the United States than was Bryce; his image of America is certainly not a flattering one. But he remained a liberal and a believer in democracy; he never had his main work translated into Russian, reportedly because he would not furnish reaction with cheap arguments. And he lived to see his hopes fulfilled as far as

Russia was concerned. He returned to his homeland after the 1905 Revolution and was elected a member of the first democratic Duma.

These are stories with happy endings. But there were other tensions beneath the surface. There were more violent forces than those that were faced by the old liberals and reflected in academic staffs. And these forces were soon going to demonstrate their power. The enigmas of post-bellum America puzzled a Europe which itself was no less riddled with contrasts and often saw its own distorted face in the American mirror. These contrasts, which made America a symbol of Europe's division, burst into the open in the cataclysmic period which began in 1914.

3. America at Europe's Crossroads (1918–1945)

I N THE parade of the victorious Allied troops in December, 1918, under the Arc de Triomphe in Paris, the various detachments marched in alphabetical order according to the official names of their nations. But an exception was made of the regiment of General John Pershing: it did not march under the "United States" but under "America," leaving it to the Americans to open the parade of triumph.

This arrangement emphasized that it was the American Expeditionary Force which had tipped the scale in the largest military conflict the world had seen. But even more, it sharply underscored the new position held by the United States generally in the world that had emerged from the debris of the battlefields. The rise of the United States to world power was a main result of the war; and it was to influence deeply the entire interrelationship of the nations of the globe—even in the tiny sector which is our subject here.

The American position of strength in the postwar world was only in part due to its display of military and economic strength; it was no less of a psychological nature. The entrance of America on the side of the Allies in their darkest hour and the tremendous war contribution of the United States created a feeling of gratitude, mixed with a kind of embarrassment about European prewar negligence and condescension. The ability of President Wilson to place the issues of the struggle in a larger perspective strengthened the feeling of unity and purpose. This American emotional impact was followed up, as soon as hostilities ended, by an increasing cultural influence, which was supported by new media of mass communication, from the movies and talkies to the radio and the comics; and starting with the middle 1920's a new American literature emerged and almost overnight made its impact felt everywhere by its poignant mixture of simplicity and art. Even in scholarship, the United States gained a position of leadership in several branches of research after the war. And this cultural maturation was further deepened from the 1920's on, by the contribution of American studies in America itself, a fresh and many-sided scholarly analysis of what the American tradition really means.

From its very beginning this postwar expansion of the United States had many negative aspects: it revived traditional doubts and created new frictions. The closeness of contact made America a part of Europe's everyday existence; and the intimacy did not always make for good will. The dream of American leadership in the brave democratic world was soon replaced by the reality of American complacency and isolationism in the 1920's. The negative impact was strengthened by the vulgar and commercialized kind of American mass civilization that only too often was broadcast to the world by the movies; and even the new American school of fiction frequently created a similar impression by its scathing criticism of American life. This image of America came as a godsend to European postwar pessimism; and there were intellectual vogues in Europe which made it only too tempting to generalize on the American experience. The myopic historicism of the positivists was increasingly being supplanted, in the postwar generation, by a new urge toward synthesis, almost at any cost, in universal systems of speculation. To many Europeans the mounting impact of American technical mass civilization began to fit into the philosophical image of a world process, which appeared as even more ominous because of Europe's weakening power to influence it.

But in Western Europe this negative trend was still only one thread in a larger pattern. Generally, criticism was apt to strengthen rather than weaken the growing interest in America and the concern with American problems; and from the 1930's on pessimism was partly countered, as far as European democratic opinion was concerned, by the reform movement of the New Deal in the United States. As a result, the urge to study America, which had steadily gained in intensity since the Civil War, was further strengthened after the conclusion of hostilities in 1918. Still, it was often tied to a general progressive and liberal ideology, as it had been in the past; in a world of rapid change America added fresh aspects to the European democratic myth. And these studies were no longer an academic concern alone but had bearing upon the education of the masses which were to dominate the new society.

In the most general sense the growth of American studies thus became a part of the efforts after the war to readjust European education. In some nations American studies came to be connected with basic issues within this process. Everywhere, the movement was supported by widening intellectual and educational contacts across the ocean, an increased exchange of books, ideas, and staff. In more and more countries such efforts now became a part of government policy; the great school reforms in the middle 1920's in both France and Germany had bearing even upon American studies. Similar trends appeared in the universities, both in established subjects and in new ones, such as American literature, which now suddenly acquired academic rank. A number of specialized chairs, libraries, and institutes were established in the service of the new work.

Beyond this concern with the subject itself, American

Civilization studies also began to make themselves felt as an influence in the field of methods. The new and general interest in comparative and structural analysis tended to break the bonds of specialization and embrace all aspects of culture in a global view. American material proved to be of special relevance to such ideas.

Even now, these reforms did not have the character of a revolution. There was yet much of thoughtless conservatism and snobbery to cope with, particularly with regard to the dreaded American pronunciation. There was more of discussion than of results, of regulations on paper than of actual work. Behind this inertia there was a deeper default. It was the period of the *trahison des clercs,* the "treason of the intellectuals," when in a number of European countries the universities sadly isolated themselves from the demands of society and left the world to its fate; even American studies were bound to suffer from this attitude. But as a whole, the forward movement was striking all through the period, and almost everywhere in Western Europe.

In Great Britain, the war and its aftermath were accompanied by a breakup of the social pattern, which made large-scale educational reform unavoidable. The new position of the United States made itself felt from the very beginning; there was a growing awareness of the problem, and not only among so-called "progressive" educators. But still a good deal remained of what a British critic in 1937 called "the silent kind of bigotry" about America; and the movement for a change temporarily lost some of its impetus in the decade of Stanley Baldwin.

With regard to the schools, more general reforms were facilitated by the introduction, in 1917, of the British Certificate Leaving Examination. While there were still eight independent examination boards in the United Kingdom, possibilities were at least opened for admitting new subjects in larger areas, and in the early twenties American history began to appear in the set examination papers. At the same time a number of schools (among them some famous public schools such as Eton and Winchester) began to teach American history in a regular way. But such experiments were not yet typical; and on a larger scale they were hindered by the narrowness of the traditional textbooks. A survey of thirty-one such books in history used in 1939 in British secondary schools showed that the American Civil War was mentioned in only six of them, America's contribution in the First World War in four, and Abraham Lincoln and Woodrow Wilson in two. In a similar way the geography books still gave much detail on British Guiana and Sarawak, but very little on the United States. In classes of English, American texts began to be recommended for home reading. But this was all extracurricular; and in the background loomed "the infectious accents of Hollywood, which are subtly corrupting the tastes and habits of the rising generation."

It was now quite widely felt that what was done in the American field in the schools was all too little. In the late 1930's there were strong public complaints in England regarding the "colossal" ignorance about the United States in secondary education, and a good deal of planning for reform was done on paper; but it was only the war itself that put these plans into effect.

The universities offered the same picture or even worse, as far as American literature was concerned. But a different story has to be told when it comes to American history, American government, and American economic life. Here the 1920's and 1930's in Great Britain represent the great turning point. The shift was made possible by the growing assistance of American visitors, and also sometimes of American donors. But decisive was the emergence of a new and talented generation of British scholars with American interests, such as H. H. Bellot, Denis W. Brogan, Harold J. Laski, and many others.

Organized work was facilitated by the successive establishment of the Harmsworth Chair at Oxford, the Commonwealth Fund Chair and a lectureship at London, an endowed lectureship at St. Andrews, and in 1944 the Pitt Chair at Cambridge, all in American history (the Oxford and Cambridge chairs are for Americans). But equally important was the arrangement of regular teaching in connection with set papers in a number of other British universities in the 1920's and 1930's, in American history, geography, economics, and institutions. The University of London began building up in its Institute of Historical Research what is now the finest bibliographical tool in Europe for investigations in American history. Independent research in the subject got under way, and had its tempting program laid out by Professor H. H. Bellot: no longer was American history to be a "separate national story to be laid arbitrarily alongside the national history of Great Britain, but an integral and vital part of the history of all those areas, European and American alike, which border upon the North Atlantic."

This development was duplicated in postwar France. The fellowship-in-arms with the United States was a great emotional experience to the French. A whole literature of Franco-American friendship came into existence during the war, emphasizing the common heritage of the two nations; and a practical result of the military operations was the establishment of the great American Library in Paris, which was originally based on books donated to the American Expeditionary Forces. This general interest received fresh impetus from the new American literature, which in part was felt as a kind of Parisian product and—in the words of Jean-Paul Sartre—represented the greatest literary experience in France between 1929 and 1939.

Decisive was the development at the Sorbonne, which normally has close connections with the central authorities in French education. During the war the University arranged lectures by Firmin Roz, that old friend of America, on "American Idealism" and on "Washington and Lincoln"; and in 1917 a lectureship of "American Literature and Civilization" was established, the first teaching position in an American subject to become permanent in a European university. With American assistance this post was made into a full professorship, and a lectureship was added, in the 1920's. In his inaugural address the first incumbent of the American chair, Charles Cestre, announced a research program of concentric investigations, guided by the methods of history, psychology, and the social sciences, and directed toward American Civilization as a living whole.

Under the leadership of M. Cestre, American studies swiftly developed within the framework established before the war. Emphasis was now on literature. In the program for the *agrégation,* there was an American section about every two years; and for the first time in Europe the work showed the modern approach to American letters. (Among set papers in the interwar years there were such as the "Secularization of Puritanism in New England," "New Psychology and New Morals in Willa Cather and O'Neill," and "The American Regionalist Novel in the 20th Century.") In addition, the French in 1918 established the first specialized American examination in Europe, a "Certificate of American Literature and Civilization," with detailed requirements. During the interwar years this certificate existed only at the universities of Paris and Lille, and it could not be used as a part of the ordinary school examinations; but it was to be of extreme importance later.

This gradual expansion in the curricula was accompanied by a similar growth in teaching. The Collège de France established a full chair in American Civilization in the early 1930's, and so did the Ecole Pratique des Hautes Etudes in American history for a few years. In the universities, lecturing under the program was extensive; particularly in geography, English, literature, and modern history, American courses were given by many of the full professors. Four French universities in the interwar years changed the title of their chairs of "English" to "English and American" literature and civilization. Doctoral theses on American subjects became relatively frequent. And this activity was paralleled by an impressive amount of independent research in practically all fields of American life. In the study of American literature, no other nation outside the United States has made a similar contribution. These literary studies had their center in the *Revue anglo-américaine*.

In French secondary schools, English became the leading modern language after the war, as German had been before. In the new plans dating from 1925 emphasis was now very much on the study of "civilization"; the United States was included in considerable detail in one of the final classes, and special textbooks appeared for this purpose. For various reasons the reform was not very effective in the interwar years; but it was to be re-emphasized by the Second World War.

A similar development, but even more momentous in its general import, took place at the same time in Germany.

The defeat in the First World War led to the downfall of the political system of the Empire, and also seriously disrupted Germany's social structure and its traditional standards. In its state of confusion the nation chose to base its future on the Western ideals of democratic progressivism which had struggled so hard for their survival in the German past. Circumstances were not promising. The economic situation was desperate; and the German democratic state met with little co-operation from the West. This notwithstanding, the task did not seem impossible. German liberals again turned their eyes toward the Anglo-Saxon nations; and the United States here came to play a part as it had never done before. Economic and cultural ties were soon re-established. The postwar impact of all forms of American Civilization on Germany proved amazing; and it was accompanied by a lively discussion of America in the most general terms.

With regard to schools and universities, the place of American material became a point in that sweeping pedagogical debate which was typical of the Weimar Republic. It was widely felt that the old school system carried a heavy responsibility for Germany's downfall. The search for a new educational philosophy was deeply influenced by new general trends and slogans in the scholarship of the 1920's—sociology, typology, structuralism, Gestalt psychology, *Geistesgeschichte*, *Kulturmorphologie*—aiming at a more integrated and synthetic conception of man and his culture. These ideas were not applied to the study of Germany alone. Even during the war itself it was maintained that one of Germany's basic shortcomings had been its failure to understand other nations. After the war, programs were formulated for a new *Auslandkunde*, which fused the methods of many sciences into an all-inclusive "interpretation of the soul of a nation." From their very beginnings these ideas met with severe criticism, which pointed to the immanent dangers of vague generalization. But the new trend represented a sound reaction against the narrowness of previous generations, and it had considerable following among the scholarly youth.

Within this framework the study of America acquired fresh importance. The entrance of the United States into the war had made the Germans realize with a shock how completely they had been out of touch with American realities; more solid American studies were declared to be an "urgent cultural need." And a new generation of scholars was now ready to do the job. The movement was headed by Friedrich Schönemann, just back from Harvard. In his famous manifesto in 1921 Schönemann raised the demands of a specialized discipline of *Amerikakunde*—not a remote corner of the study of English any more, but a branch of a new, integrated, and interdisciplinary study of civilization, closely tied to the social sciences.

This manifesto, and those of other enthusiasts, became part of a heated debate over the aims and means of such studies, a debate which in many ways is still relevant. Largely speaking, the new ideas were not accepted: the framework of both general and American studies remained traditional. But the influence of the discussion is felt down to this day; and the exchange of opinions generally strengthened the German willingness to increase the range of all studies of civilization, including that of the United States.

In the secondary schools the famous Prussian instructions of 1925 were deeply influenced by the ideals of the *Kulturkunde*: particularly in the field of English, the plans now included a surprising amount of American material taken from many fields of cultural life and treated from general points of view. In some respects the approach showed the dangers of the new structuralism. But taken as a whole, the plan was sensational and exerted a strong influence in Germany even outside Prussia. The subject was handled with great seriousness; thus, an impressive co-operative *Handbuch der Amerikakunde* for teachers appeared in 1931.

The universities proceeded with more caution. There was no tendency to recognize American studies as a separate field; as before they had to survive as a voluntary specialization within the established subjects. But with these qualifications, the work showed a surprising growth. While there was no full chair before Hitler, a number of other teaching positions offered opportunities to the young "Americanists"; and many of *die alten Herren* went into American studies as well.

This fresh interest was reflected in the lecture lists. During the Weimar period from 1919–33 the twenty-three German universities at the time announced an average of one specialized American course each per semester. The larger institutions sometimes had impressive programs, in particular Göttingen, Hamburg, Leipzig, and for a short while Münster and Berlin. Hamburg, toward the end of the period, announced four to five specialized American courses per semester (in addition, of course, to American work in general teaching); during the winter term of 1928–29, before the depression set in, the University of Berlin announced eleven separate American courses.

Almost as important as the quantity of these lectures was their wide coverage. As a sign of the times, American literature now moved into first place, as it did simultaneously in France. But the subject did not occupy more than one quarter of the courses; the remainder was devoted to practically all other aspects of American life. In the approach, the ideas of the new integrated *Kulturkunde* were now often apparent, and not always to their advantage; some courses had titles of untranslatable vagueness, such as American *Geistesverfassung* and *Kulturgerichtetheit*. But as a whole there was a laudable effort to judge American Civilization no more by British or European yardsticks alone, but by its own standards.

There was a similar growth in research; in the year 1930 alone, German universities accepted thirty theses on American Civilization. The production of books and articles was impressive, and no less many-sided than was teaching; only contemporary France can be mentioned in comparison.

The general weakness of the German system remained. As before, activity largely depended on the temper of the professor; in small universities with limited staffs American work often remained insignificant. But taken together on all levels of education, these American studies during the few years of the Weimar Republic probably represent the most hopeful development in the entire history of the discipline in Europe before 1945. And they formed part of something that was even more important than scholarship: the effort to create a democratic Germany. The import of the failure of that effort was soon to be felt by the entire world.

A similar story could be told about a number of the small democratic nations of Europe in this period. In various forms these nations continued adding to the American sector in their schools and universities, and research on the United States and its civilization continued to develop as part of a peaceful growth where America had still retained much of its traditional symbolic value.

But this was only half of the story—perhaps not even the more important half. Beneath this seemingly smooth surface there were immense accumulated tensions. They had made themselves felt as subterranean quakes and rumblings since the time of the Paris Commune. In the latter part of the interwar period they erupted with irresistible force; in their consequences they created a completely new constellation of world power, which is likely to last even after our time, and which deeply affected even the position of the United States.

Bourgeois liberalism and laissez-faire had solved many of the political problems of democracy. But throughout Europe, the social and economic ills inherited from the past had not been cured, or had been only partly so; and in the less well-developed areas, which existed under the continued pressure of semifeudal social structures, the process of change had hardly begun as yet. The war and postwar upheavals, followed by the depression, brought these problems to the fore everywhere; and here the United States of the 1920's had little to offer. In a number of Western European countries the Social Democrats now came to represent the power of progress, and sometimes took over the government. In spite of their different economic philosophy most of the Socialists retained their sympathy with America and its heritage of political democracy and intellectual freedom. But in states with more violent internal contrasts and with less established liberal traditions, the tension now gave new strength to latent forces which were frankly anti-democratic.

These forces could only have been countered by swift and radical reforms. But neither the United States nor the other Western powers showed much understanding of the situation, and in a shortsighted fear of any kind of social change they often refused to support their real friends. As a result, the postwar years saw the birth in many parts of Europe of victorious totalitarian movements which masked their true character by a revolutionary ideology and which saw the United States no longer as the symbol of liberty but of reaction. In this new chapter of the European myth-making,

American studies were to play their important part, just as they did on other premises in the democratic states.

The signal of this reversal was given during the First World War by the 1917 Revolution in Russia. The fall of Tsarism seemed to inaugurate a new era of friendship between liberal Russia and the United States. But the October Revolution and Lenin's ascendency to power soon changed the picture completely. What distinguished the Russian Communists from the traditional Western radicals was not only their ruthless cynicism, but their adherence to the general and dogmatic system of Marxism as expounded by Engels and Lenin. From the beginning this allegiance was not blind, and some freedom was allowed for experimentation. But from the adoption in 1928 of the first Five Year Plan and the emergence of Stalin as Lenin's successor, regimentation was gradually tightened. Propaganda became more and more all-embracing and efficient; and the great purges in the 1930's increased the trend toward a total subservience to the creed.

This development gradually gave America an importance in Russian life that it had never had before. Particularly after the American intervention in the Revolutionary War the Soviet leaders came to regard the United States as the main antagonist of the Soviet Union in its struggle for world Communism. In the 1930's there was still some leeway for interpretation; but the basic anti-Americanism of the Russian Government remained. It was expressed in definitive terms by Stalin as early as in 1925; in the 1930's it was gradually embodied in an official negative image of the United States. This image was expounded in the authoritative *History of the Communist Party* (1938), which long remained the "Soviet catechism for philosophical, political and historical thought." The image appeared in a number of travel books, monographs, and government-sponsored handbooks on the

United States, and step by step it became an integral part of the entire supervised publishing and news service.

This counterimage of America contained much truth; in many details it was based on Ostrogorsky's great work, which now appeared in Russian translation. But as an over-all interpretation the picture was grossly oversimplified, and often it generalized on conditions in earlier periods. (Thus, the entire reform work of the 1930's in the United States was usually passed over in silence.) At the same time, tightened control of all information made it possible to withhold from the Soviet citizen practically all material that might challenge the authorized version.

Beginning with the 1930's this image of America became of great importance even in Soviet education. At the same time, the tremendous progress of Russian schools and universities in the period made them a perfect tool for supervised political indoctrination. No thorough survey has yet been made of the place of American studies within this system at the time, but the general trend is unmistakable. On all levels and in all subjects the United States was given great attention as the outstanding example of capitalist exploitation, oppression, and aggressiveness under the mask of a fake political democracy. In the schools, the teaching of history, geography, and English offered rich American material to exemplify in a negative way the political tenets of the Party; and the case was similar in the universities, where America was treated in a spirit of complete equality with the other defendants under Marxist-Leninist law.

Even some research was done, and part of it may have been of scholarly value, particularly if the subjects did not directly touch upon the domains of propaganda. But the growing political pressure was obvious; it was demonstrated by the critical surveillance of all scholarship by the Party press, and by the rueful recantations even by outstanding scholars if they were accused of heresy.

Neither was this influence limited to Russia alone. In all European countries, growing Communist parties looked to the Soviet Union for guidance and direction; and they faithfully passed on the Soviet propaganda, including the image of the United States.

The leaders of the Soviet Union believed themselves to be working in accordance with the laws of history; they could afford to take their time. The other totalitarian movements which swept Central Europe acted at a more spasmodic pace, but their anti-Americanism was no less basic than that of the Communists. In the anarchic "philosophy" of the black and brown dictatorships, one of the unifying links was the hatred against the "eighteenth century" and its heritage of political democracy, humanitarianism and pacifism. This tradition had always been linked to America; the contrast was there from the beginning, and the inherent dynamism of the dictators led to an armed conflict with the United States in the course of a few years.

The movement first ascended to power in Italy. The country fought on the side of the Allies in the First World War, and the co-operation seemed to inaugurate a warm friendship with the United States. One fruit of this brief honeymoon was the privately donated Nelson Gay Memorial Library in Rome, which even today is an important center of American studies. But the resistance of President Wilson to Italy's territorial aspirations soon turned this pro-Americanism into its counterpart. A violent chauvinist propaganda, a succession of weak governments, and a welter of social problems left unsolved for generations paved the way for fascism, which was carried into power in 1922.

There was no doubt about the general aims of the Black

Shirts. Against the enlightened democratic ideas which had inspired Mazzini and the Italian *Risorgimento,* fascism raised the banner of dictatorship and of military conquest, eventually even of racialism; and there was no hesitation to use the methods required. At the same time, the movement showed many contradictions. It could never find a definition for itself; even its practical measures were often incoherent. There was no organized resistance against fascism in Italy, but a good deal of silent sabotage; at the same time reprisals never showed that bestiality which soon became customary north of the Alps.

The same mixture of attitudes appeared in the approach to the United States. The American heritage represented the very opposite of Mussolini's political histrionics; he early turned his propaganda against American democracy and tried to make the Nelson Gay Library into an instrument of *Kulturpolitik* in the German style. But at the same time he carried on a successful flirtation with American conservatives; and his propaganda was jerky and haphazard. The unsystematic Italians never worked out any authorized, consistent counterimage of the United States like the one which appeared in the Soviet Union, and there was no thorough screening of information. During the 1930's Italian literary critics were even able to turn modern American fiction into a powerful secret weapon against the hollowness of fascism.

This ambiguity appeared also to some extent in education. In the schools, anti-American propaganda was sometimes balanced by other measures of political expediency; thus, all Italian pupils were once ordered by Mussolini to listen to speeches on George Washington's birthday. English classes were generally instructed to pay more attention to American Civilization than before; special textbooks appeared for the purpose, and a few of them showed considerable independence. Even in the universities, some cautious American requirements were introduced, particularly in English; and there was a growth in the number of courses. The departments of political science in Italian universities showed a despicable subservience to the fascist regime. But in other departments protests were voiced once in a while, even against the distorted image of America.

As a whole, however, such inconsistencies could not change the general trend. The very atmosphere of fascism worked against the ideals and traditions of the United States. So did the spirit of the new authoritarian education; and the entrance of Italy into the war against the United States, on the side of Germany and actually under German surveillance, made this trend all-pervasive.

A parallel development took place in Portugal and Spain. In both countries liberal governments tried to carry through progressive reforms in the period; in both, this policy also involved a strengthening of ties with the English-speaking nations. But in both, dictatorship took over in the 1930's— in Spain, after the conclusion of a long civil war—and replaced the parliamentary system by totalitarian regimes, in a spirit which was far removed from that of modern America.

The organized center of these anti-democratic movements was, of course, Nazi Germany. The Weimar Government had worked under tremendous handicaps, which in the long run proved to be overwhelming. The Revolution in 1918 did not go far enough; many of the old power groups in Germany remained intact. The democratic regime had no firm hold even on the masses. When the world crisis struck in the late 1920's the Nazis skillfully used these contrasts, playing at the same time on social radicalism and on old national resentments and uncertainties. German intellectuals, above all in the universities, showed their complete inadequacy in the situation, and sounded no warning until it was too late. The Nazi ideology was a façade put up in order to disguise the basic nihilism of the movement; in higher party circles the gospel was not even treated too respectfully. But some of its tenets were important enough, and they fitted into a system of world history centered around Nazi Germany and its Führer and intended to propagate their ideas. In this queer construction, the United States, past and present, was bound to play a considerable part, as can be studied in the authoritative works of Hitler and Arthur Rosenberg, and in the reports of Hermann Rauschning.

The hatred of the Western traditions was no less violent among the Nazis than it was among the Fascists. The new order could not come about without conquering the United States both in the world at large and in the minds of the Germans. The Nazi image of America was to serve this purpose, putting into a system the most curious fancies about America invented by German nationalist historians and seasoning them with a dash of Madison Grant and Lothrop Stoddard. The core of the "mongrel" American nation, according to these theories, was the population of "Nordic" blood, from the Norse Vikings to the German immigrants. These elements had always represented the sound strand of Americanism; they suffered a sad defeat in the Civil War, but they were going to return victorious in a second American Revolution led by the Nazi German-Americans, who would then push back all the inferior races, repudiate democracy, and make the United States join Germany in the world domination by the Aryans.

This image of America was never worked into a system as elaborate as that which was developed at the same time in Soviet Russia. But in outline it was clear enough, and it became a part of that amazing propaganda machine which was one of the most original creations of Nazism. A directed news service began feeding the nation appropriate information, and nothing else, about the United States. American books for translation were carefully screened, literature on America that did not fit in was removed from the libraries, and a new generation of believing "scholars" began to produce that new interpretation of America which would fill the Party's bill.

The Nazis proved to have only a few years to realize these ideas before war came, and many plans never went into effect; but their intentions can be studied in detail. This also holds true of education. In the schools, new regulations of 1938 prescribed how to "mold the National Socialist Man" by a "rigorous selection of facts." Here the United States played an extensive part, both in history and English, a good deal more than it had done under Weimar. The subject was taken very seriously. There was an extensive literature of specialized textbooks on America for German secondary schools, and large chapters on the subject were included in the handbooks of classroom technique; the universities of Berlin and Göttingen announced courses for future teachers on the methods of introducing *Amerikakunde* in the schools. But the approach to the subject represented nothing but a grotesque caricature of the "synthetic" ideas of the Weimar period twisted into the service of the Party ideology.

A similar development took place in teaching in the universities. General American requirements were added to, as they were in the schools; in English, new regulations in 1940 for the first time made it possible to exchange British for American material on the same level. The number of American courses continued to increase in all fields, and particularly after the outbreak of the war in 1939. During the war years the University of Berlin offered an average of eighteen specialized American courses per semester, and in the one summer term of 1942 as many as thirty weekly hours.

But this growth in quantity corresponded to a steady decline in quality. Many old staff members were discharged or steered away from the ticklish subject. A few of them tried to keep up standards of criticism—to quote a German student, "saying it without saying it." But others shamelessly denied their past and joined in the propaganda; so did a number of young scholars. More than half of all the specialized American courses were given at the University of Berlin, many of them in a special propaganda faculty. The titles of the courses were often revealing, such as: American psychology in the light of the *Volkscharacterologie,* or: the "National Biology" of American history.

Research and popularization were undertaken at the same hectic pace; an average of about fifty German books a year appeared on the United States during the Nazi period. Some of these books obviously belonged in the field of decent scholarship. But the bulk of them were propaganda for home consumption, describing the United States in terms of the new Teutonic millennium that was just around the corner.

This activity, of course, was not activated by a search for truth, but was a part of German power politics, in preparation for the inevitable war. These plans also involved the incorporation of the smaller states of Central Europe into the Nazi system.

Many of these nations after 1918 saw the rise of strong popular movements which tried to solve the urgent social problems along democratic lines. In some of these states such as Estonia, Rumania, and Yugoslavia, interest in America was active and the first feeble efforts were made to build up American studies. This was the case in particular in Austria. The country had been treated without much foresight by the victors in 1918, but it undauntedly tried to rebuild its existence in a democratic spirit, and in the 1920's and 1930's gave America a decent place in its educational system. The same development was even more pronounced in Czechoslovakia, which owed its new existence to the West; there was a monument to President Wilson in Prague from 1928 to 1941, and an independent American Institute. In the 1930's the Czechs made the teaching of American literature and history compulsory in the universities, and a good many specialized courses were given both at Bratislava and Prague.

But all such efforts were doomed. The democratic movements in these nations worked against heavy odds; and they received little encouragement from the West. In the 1930's the democratic regimes succumbed one by one to a wave of totalitarianism modeled on Germany and often directly supported from Berlin. The Czechs and Austrians enjoyed a brief respite, but only until the Nazis felt strong. The rape of Austria and the betrayal of Czechoslovakia in 1938 were the starting signals for the war which Hitler—in his own words— "would unleash before he grew too old," and which was intended to wrest world leadership from the West.

America was deeply involved in these European complications on the eve of the Second World War. Politically the United States was still neutral and aloof, wrapped in the shroud of isolationism; actually it was at Europe's crossroads. In the lining-up for battle, images and ideologies were massed against each other as much as men and machines. Here, America's spiritual past and future were at stake no less than its political existence.

Thus it was natural that after its awakening to realities in the Second World War the United States gradually became a leader in the great democratic coalition, where the most heterogeneous powers were forced together to meet the immediate danger. As a result of this conflict the United States was placed in a new position of strength and faced with a burden of unparalleled international responsibility. These are decisive factors in the postwar world, a world in which our generation must exist whether we like it or not.

To focus this welter of contrasts on the portraits of individuals is only possible by gross oversimplification. It must even be unfair; many of the best men of the period have suffered or perished in silence, ground to death by conflicting forces. But even a few glimpses without many details may symbolize the two main camps before 1945.

There is on one side Bernard Fay, brilliant historian of the Franco-American fellowship in the period of the Revolution, many-sided chronicler of the American past, full professor of American civilization at the Collège de France in the 1930's, and full-fledged traitor and collaborator with the Germans from 1940 on, a man who in 1960 is still physically alive but morally dead. There was from another nation the recently deceased Friedrich Schönemann, founder of the discipline of "Americanistics" in Germany, full professor of the field in Berlin from 1936, author of perhaps the most thorough and rounded analysis of American Civilization produced in Europe in this century—and from 1933 on a subservient Nazi, who rewrote his books in accordance with the official demands, and tried in vain to regain his position after 1945, by changing his books a second time.

On the other side, there are those who followed a different road. There was Charles Cestre, teacher and professor of American literature and civilization at the Sorbonne from 1917 on, a tireless interpreter of American literature and American ideas in books and translations, who down to 1944 continued serving the good cause in occupied Paris. There is still Denis W. Brogan, spirited critic and commentator on American mores, leading scholar on American political and social institutions, about which he has taught at great British universities since the 1920's, and all through the war years and after a builder and fortifier of Anglo-Saxon amity on the basis of factual knowledge. There was the late Italian scholar Gennaro Mondaini who, around the turn of the century, wrote great works on the Negro problem and on the rise of the American republic, and in his old age, as a professor of economic history in Rome, had his American course forbidden by Mussolini. There is, still, the Norwegian social democrat Halvdan Koht, who came to the United States for the first time in 1908 and ever since has taught and written on American history at the University of Oslo, and is the founder of American studies in Norway. He was the Minister of Foreign Affairs to receive, and reject, Hitler's ultimatum to Norway in 1940; and he used his war years of exile in the United States to write the first general survey of the American impact on Europe.

If this is a picture of great and contradictory variety, it is the variety of the time itself. The story will be none the simpler when we study the concluding chapter of it.

4. The Second Discovery (1945–Present)

I N ONE of the many occupied nations of Europe during the Second World War a woman sometimes managed to hear on her hidden, illegal radio some of the great war speeches of President Franklin D. Roosevelt. She once said: "It's amazing about that President of the United States. He is speaking across thousands of miles of ocean; and still, he seems to speak directly to me, about everything we have to suffer here."

This little anecdote is not only a testimony to the human power of appeal in Franklin Roosevelt's personality; it also tells something about that leadership in a struggling world which the United States took on during the war. Once again, to uncounted millions, America was "the Beacon of Liberty," the hope and promise of a world better than that of the firing squads and the gas chambers.

When the day of liberation finally dawned, moreover, this moral strength of the United States was equaled by a physical power, which in comparison to that of Europe appeared almost overwhelming. This situation and its implications were matched by a new attitude among the Americans themselves. The war experience had created a widespread understanding in America of the new rôle of the United States in the world. This thinking on a global scale was implemented by the American government, as the situation changed, by international organizations on a vast scale, diplomatic, military, and economic; and these efforts were supplemented by a new policy of cultural co-operation. A huge system of American information libraries (some of them almost scholarly in character) made American source material available in countless places where a well-rounded American book collection had never been seen before. Immense quantities of American printed matter of all kinds poured into the European libraries as gifts; and by acts of Congress exchanges of staffs across the ocean were made possible on an unprecedented scale. The hundreds of American university professors teaching their own civilization all over Europe after the war may well be compared, in effort, if not in results, to the exodus of Greek scholars from fallen Constantinople five hundred years ago.

These planned activities were equaled—or more than equaled—by an undirected and no less overwhelming invasion of Europe by all other forms of American Civilization. The elimination of distance was symbolized in the European editions of American daily newspapers and the world circulation of American paperbacks at all levels of literature. For the first time in history the two great halves of the Western world began to approach each other, in some fields at least, as if the Atlantic were not there.

Much of this activity sprang from an urge on the part of the Americans to explain their nation and its problems to the Europeans. And this urge met with a similar concern on the European side of the Atlantic. With France and Germany obviously weakened, cultural Europe more and more turned to the English-speaking nations (since the war English is now taught as the first or second foreign language almost everywhere), and great attention was given to the United States. In the schools, reforms to introduce American studies or to strengthen their position began in some countries during the war itself, and they continued widely after hostilities ended. The universities followed the same lead, organizing definite American programs in most of the countries of Europe. In the 1950's the general economic recovery made this trend even more marked than it had been in the 1940's.

This international movement still left much to be desired. But, both in regard to its geographical extent and to the energy involved, it appears impressive, and no less so because it is now known only in part. If it is compared to the efforts before 1939, it may be tempting to speak of a Second Discovery of the United States: never before has American Civilization been studied on this scale.

But from the very beginning, this discovery was used for other than purely educational purposes. Ideally, organized American studies should contribute to the sober analysis of the United States in the European mind; actually, even scholarly American work soon became engaged anew in a genuine battle of the myths, and the old cleavages reappeared.

During the holocaust of the war the people of the Western nations—and quite particularly the Americans—had hoped for a new democratic unity after the war. But even before hostilities ended these hopes proved futile. Fascism and Nazism were eliminated, but the conditions which created them were not. To millions of Europeans, traditional political democracy still offered no answer to their needs, let alone the "American Way" with its totally different background. And behind these European issues loomed the rising masses of mankind in Asia and Africa, which were unimpressed by both Europe's and America's achievement, and looked about for their own solutions to their staggering problems.

There was a resurgence of deeper cultural doubts. As the new forms of international technical and commercial civilization spanned the globe—as Coca-Cola stands sprang up in the Arabian desert and Bing Crosby crooned from Palermo to the North Cape—there was a deepening concern in white and colored races alike on behalf of indigenous values and traditional standards. There was a growing tendency to resist the restless efficiency and enameled smoothness of the new technical culture; and more often than not this culture was introduced under an American trade-mark and backed by American capital. This cultural anti-Americanism was found almost everywhere in Europe; often it played off the more traditional civilization of Great Britain against its American counterpart. Such criticism might be combined with both good will and understanding toward the United States. But it might also serve those who, for various reasons, wanted to eliminate the American influence altogether.

After the Nazis were gone, the active center of these negative forces became the Soviet Union. During the war, the West wooed the Russians intensively, and they responded with a sort of grudging friendliness. There was some relaxation of control in the Soviet Union, and even a more balanced picture of the United States was occasionally allowed to appear. But there was no basic change of attitude; and after the cessation of hostilities Soviet policy stiffened again almost immediately. The unmistakable sign of the future was the decision of the Russians to remain in all the countries they had overrun in 1944–45. In the interest of self-preservation even the Western powers had to organize in NATO, which was largely built on American military strength, leaving the world divided into the two armed camps of the Cold War, which is still on.

Parallel with this political alignment, anti-Americanism again became the official policy in the Soviet Union, and even more violently so than before. In famous speeches in 1946–47, Russian leaders like Zhdanov and Malenkov declared war against all "deference to the foreign cultures of the West," in particular that of the United States, the symbol of capitalist decadence. An anti-American propaganda campaign of baffling virulence was unleashed, not only in the Soviet Union but throughout Communist-dominated Eastern Europe and Asia. As many times before in history, the attitude toward the United States appeared as a main point in the division of hostile philosophies, but now on a world scale.

From our special point of view, however, the decisive fact is that within each of the two opposing camps in the world today there is about the same eagerness to "study" the United States (if the word "study" is used in a liberal sense). The importance of the American phenomenon together with the necessity of understanding and interpreting it is equally realized in both groups. The ultimate goals of this work vary to the point of excluding each other; sometimes it is hard to realize that it is actually the same United States that is being studied. But that very discovery is going on, undauntedly, and in all seriousness, both east and west of the Iron Curtain. There is also a similar activity within the bloc of the "neutralists."

In the Communist zone of Europe the lead is in all respects taken by the Soviet Union. What distinguishes these Soviet American studies is not the number of mistakes or distortions in detail; prejudice and misjudgments about America abound in Western Europe as well. Nor is it the application of Marxist theory, which often has proved an excellent hypothesis for research both in Europe and the United States. It is the fact that in the Soviet-dominated zone one single image of the United States is the only interpretation that is officially permitted; this image, and this alone, is expounded by all means of communication, and the individual largely has to accept it (or to pretend that he does). In this juggernaut of general propaganda, education is only one spoke in the wheel; and to imagine any independence on its part on this, or on any other point of basic importance, makes no more sense than to imagine one spoke taking a different course from the others.

How important a place the American material holds within this system of indoctrination can be gauged from the detailed timetables of Soviet schools. Geography, with emphasis on economic conditions, takes much space in Russian classes. The United States is treated in a summary way in the sixth year of secondary school, and more thoroughly in the ninth year, where out of eighty-one class hours twelve are devoted to the Western Hemisphere and six of these to the United States. The program marshals an impressive array of geographic facts. But emphasis is political; in the background looms the American "designs for world domination."

In American history, the period down to the Civil War is studied in the eighth year, and the following period to 1917 in the ninth year (five hours are devoted to the latter subject); the period after 1917 apparently does not come in for separate consideration, obviously because it might disturb the established image. The selection of material can be studied in detail in the textbooks, where Marx, Engels, Lenin, and Stalin are constantly referred to as supreme authorities on particulars of American geography and history. Often these details are quite amusing—for example, the disproportionate importance attributed to General Sherman's march to the sea, because Marx had stated in an article that it would be wise for the Union armies to undertake exactly that strategic move. The gradual hardening of the propaganda after the war can be followed in the new directives for teachers issued in the 1950's, with their violent language against the American "imperialistic bandits."

Of particular interest is the study of English, which is now taught from the fourth or fifth class on, and which in the number of pupils is second only to German. The available primers and anthologies show a curious mixture of neutral material and propaganda; apparently Dickens is still regarded as excellent source material for present-day social England, while Harriet Beecher Stowe plays the same part for America. Knowing how little information of other kinds is being admitted to the Soviet Union, it is hard to imagine how a Russian teacher, working with these books, could give any balanced image of the United States, even if he wanted to and dared to.

A similar situation is typical in the universities. All Russian students receive extensive and compulsory training in Marxism-Leninism, and in philosophy and world history in the same spirit. In addition they also have to study one Western modern language (sometimes two); and apparently about half of the students now choose English. The United States obviously plays a considerable part in this education, both in many of the preparatory courses and, in more detail, in a number of the specialized faculties. In addition the Soviet Union has large government institutes for world history, world politics, world economy, and foreign languages. In all these institutions a good deal of time is devoted to the United States; for instance, the Maxim Gorky Institute of World Literature has a number of specialists in American letters. Allegedly, the University of Moscow at one time even had a special professorship in "American Imperialism."

This title, however, whether authentic or not, may also indicate the real purpose of this entire activity. In Western Europe, most universities on principle encourage a diversity of opinion, on the United States as on everything else. The Soviet system recognizes no such ideal; on the contrary, diversity of opinion is regarded as the supreme sign of rotten Western objectivism. Like the schools, even the Russian universities largely devote themselves to the application of preconceived ideas, in accordance with directives which, in the past, were often laid down by vote of the Party Congress. No doubt academic teaching in the Soviet Union therefore largely presents and expatiates upon the authorized image of the United States, as do all media of directed propaganda.

The same obviously holds true for the bulk of Russian research on America, which is not negligible. Much of this material, even in the scholarly journals, is rankly propagandist. Suppression and so-called revision of scholarly literature has been daily fare, even in the American field. A history of American literature was projected in 1946; but the first volume proved to be too "objective," and the second volume has never appeared.

In the late 1940's, this Russian system of American studies was also gradually introduced into the other states of Eastern Europe. This process met with considerable resistance. After the war ended, several of the nations in question established liberal governments in the Western spirit; a few of them even made pathetic efforts to build up American studies as a symbol of their Western allegiance. But this resistance was short-lived. One by one the new regimes were replaced by local Communist cliques supported by Russian arms. Cultural life was similarly geared to that of the Soviet Union; Russian was everywhere made the first and compulsory foreign language, and Russian textbooks and journals became the cornerstone of teaching and research. In this monolithic system, the United States from the late 1940's onwards took on the same position as it held in Russia. By 1950 America was the subject of a continuous stream of vituperation in all media of communication, from Bucharest to the Branden-burg Gate.

There is no reason to retell this story in detail; as an example it may suffice to choose East Germany (the so-called "German Democratic Republic"). In East Germany, as in most of these states, there was an initial period of caution which was reflected even in American work; as late as in 1947 the East German secondary school students still studied the intellectual life of the United States by reading, among others, the works of Emerson, Carl Schurz, and James Truslow Adams. But beginning in 1948, education followed the political shift. Studies on all levels were made subservient to propaganda and indoctrination, even including "political autobiographies" presented by the pupils; and the well-known Russian material, including the image of the "cannibalistic" United States, was introduced on all levels.

In East German schools these American studies seem to be a good deal more thorough than the corresponding studies in Russia. In geography, for instance, the United States is studied in the tenth class for eighteen hours. In history there are six hours, divided in accordance with the Russian plan. English is optional (Russian is the compulsory foreign language). But the list of obligatory reading pays much attention to America, with drastic political bias; main emphasis is on Tom Paine, Mark Twain's *The Gilded Age,* Theodore Dreiser, and Howard Fast, who until his condemnation of the Soviet policy in Hungary was the leading name in modern American literature throughout Eastern Europe.

The universities were made a part of the same system. In history the United States is not mentioned specifically in the curricula, probably because treatment is sufficient in general courses; but in geography, North America alone is studied for two weekly lecture hours throughout one semester. In the department of English, the equality of British and American material is emphasized to the point that even the common language is consistently referred to as "English-American." The time devoted to each subject is carefully laid down, and the American side is well taken care of; thus, American geography and history have 51 hours of teaching, American literature 246 hours, while 322 hours are used on "English-American" special problems.

For these reasons, there is a good deal of specialized teaching on America in East German universities, particularly in the departments of English. In Berlin, there are two professors of American studies and an American Institute with a good-sized library. Two other universities have similar institutes; and in three other universities there are chairs of "English and American literature." Of doctoral dissertations on literature in the English language accepted in East Germany from 1945 to 1959 exactly 50 per cent were on American subjects.

The gist of this activity is, however, clear. There has been continued resistance against the regime in East Germany. It is notable that, long after the Communists took over, the reading lists of British and American literature in the universities were not politically biased, as were those in the schools. But the older professors who tried to stick to traditional standards are increasingly being replaced by a younger and more reliable generation. The political pressure on the universities is tremendous, as is the isolation from the West. This situation is also bound to influence research. Quite a few books appear on American Civilization in East Germany, and since 1953 there has been a scholarly journal for "Anglistics and Americanistics." But outside the neutral field of philology it is hard to avoid propaganda.

The same story was repeated in all the other satellite states. Hungary tried to organize an American Institute during the brief period before the Communists took over. In Czechoslovakia, where American studies had long traditions, there were regular American courses by appointed teachers in the same years, and a great enthusiasm, which is movingly described by the late F. O. Matthiessen, visiting professor at Prague in 1947–48. But this entire effort was wiped out under the Communist regime and the authorized system introduced instead.

The great exception is, of course, Yugoslavia. The Yugoslavs were never Russian satellites. From the beginning they introduced the Russian system of indoctrination, including the stereotyped anti-Americanism; even today many Yugoslav anthologies of English and American literature, for instance, look exactly like corresponding works in East Germany. But beginning with Marshal Tito's Declaration of Independence toward the Russians in 1948 the country struck its famous middle course of "national communism"; this trend was symbolized by the fact that the Russian language was again made optional in the schools, on par with the three great Western tongues. Tito did not join the democratic camp, but he liberalized his attitude toward the West, including the United States. Anti-American propaganda was played down; American information agencies were admitted, and more leeway was given generally to the interpretation of American culture.

Within this framework much time is devoted today to the United States in Yugoslav schools, particularly in some of the universities. At least three of them have English departments with detailed American programs, where as many as two obligatory semester courses are given in American literature. The image presented of the United States obviously is the

Communist one. But doubtless this image is being modified in Yugoslavia more than in any other Communist nation, as can be seen from the Western handbooks that are now admitted for use beside the Russian ones. Since such gradual modification is apparently the only possibility of liberalizing the Communist world at the moment, the importance of the Yugoslav experiment is self-evident.

After the death of Stalin in 1953, the prospects for a liberalization along similar lines seemed to grow everywhere in Eastern Europe; even in Russia itself anti-American propaganda became less oppressive. But none of the Communist governments seriously considered abolishing the system of indoctrination; and following the abortive revolution in Hungary, pressure increased anew. Only in Poland the shift apparently led to more lasting results. In some respects the situation in Poland today corresponds to that in Yugoslavia; most notably there is much more contact with the West than there was before. This development is also bound to influence American studies in Poland, which in 1956 were made more regular, and which have gradually been added to ever since. But whether these shifts, in Poland and elsewhere, may eventually lead to a real change of intellectual climate depends on developments which are not decided in Belgrade or Warsaw.

If, from this part of the world, we turn to the west of Europe, we are met by a picture of baffling variety. Here there is certainly no streamlining or regimentation; even in its general attitude toward the United States Western Europe runs the entire gamut, from the pious adulation of the businessman to the flippant irony of the *littérateur*. But coming from the stuffy atmosphere of Eastern Europe, one is apt to feel these cool winds as extremely refreshing.

The recent swift progress of American studies in the west has a partly political background, as it has in the east. Important in this picture are, of course, the Americans themselves—a helpful factor, and sometimes a complicating one. They have often provided the resources which started the European wheels moving. But their eagerness also once in a while shows a certain "inflationary bent"; they have sometimes exaggerated the possibilities of American studies in Europe, in particular when it comes to the establishment of a separate, integrated American discipline. The long-range importance of these suggestions can hardly be doubted. They point to some of the basic weaknesses of academic studies (not only in Europe); and they are useful as an element of fermentation. But the advocates of American studies in Europe could not stake the future of the subject on such revolutionary ideas. They have had to fight their battles within the established disciplines, demanding that America be given its proper share in traditional regulations; and it is within this framework that the main progress is being made, all over Europe.

The new situation is symbolized by the changes that have taken place in Great Britain. The war finally brought home to the British that, in the words of Winston Churchill, they are forever "mixed-up together with the Americans." British education authorities went about strengthening American studies with the same determination that in 1944 created the Butler Act. During the war a series of circulars, issued by the British and Scottish Ministries of Education, urged the schools to give American material much more prominence, and to stop judging it "according to an English scale of values." Seventeen summer schools of American history for secondary school teachers were arranged by the Ministry of Education in England and Wales during the war; and they were supplemented by multifold activity and discussion in all parts of the kingdom.

The results of this movement do not affect the traditional framework. Now, as before, the British are not interested in building a uniform and coherent secondary school of the Continental type. But within the traditional "chunk system" with its voluntary specialization, American material is now growing steadily in importance. Exception has to be made for American literature. But in geography and history, almost all the examination boards now include American subjects regularly, and the subjects are often chosen from recent periods. The schools offer a good many specialized courses. In the "public," independent schools, almost a quarter of the students now study American history for twenty-four class hours or more in addition to American material in general courses.

Among the universities in the United Kingdom, practically all have now organized the study of some branch of American Civilization, and the larger universities usually present a number of papers and courses. The trend toward integration is weak in Great Britain; but individual subjects are strong. British honors students in geography, for instance, now normally attend a compulsory course of twenty-four lectures on North America. In economics and political science the growth is similar; American material occupies a full term or more in more than a dozen general British courses on government and comparative law, in addition to specialized teaching. These studies are particularly elaborate at the London School of Economics, on all levels of specialization.

American history holds the strongest position, as it always has, in Great Britain. Specialized courses are now offered and papers are being set in the subject by almost all British uni-

versities. These American lectures and papers are chosen by
an increasing number of history students; in 1954, American
history was a "significant ingredient" in the work of 44 per
cent of general (pass) students in history, and in that of 60
per cent of honors students. The importance of American
material in the program also makes chances quite good for
future scholars in the field. There are at present in British
universities more than a dozen permanent chairs for British
citizens where American Civilization is explicitly mentioned
in the title, and many more teachers teach such subjects.
The second full chair of American history and institutions
for a Briton was established in 1959 at the University of
Manchester.

At long last, even American literature is slowly penetrat-
ing the British university walls. Apparently, no American
authors except Henry James and T. S. Eliot have yet been
included in the obligatory syllabus of any British university.
But optional American survey courses have been established
after the war at two London colleges, at Manchester, and at
Nottingham, and graduate programs are under way. Since
1955, the first lectureships in American literature or American studies have been established at Aberystwyth, Manchester, and North Staffordshire, and a full chair of American
literature at Leeds; a number of other universities are planning for regular teaching in the field.

Finally, research is making headway. The times are past
when British scholars were not available for the production
of an American history; a testimony to the new activity is
the volume *British Essays on American History,* which appeared in 1957, the co-operative effort of seventeen British
scholars. Even an American literary history by a British
university man saw the light in 1954, seventy years after

John Nichol. A British Association for American Studies was founded in 1955 and is extremely active.

Moving from England to France in these matters, even today means a change of atmosphere as sudden as that which strikes the traveler crossing the English Channel from New-haven to Dieppe. In American studies as in all other subjects French education is still as consistently and pellucidly centralized as British is rambling and individualistic. But the general growth is the same.

American studies are old in France. What was needed in the schools in the postwar years was mostly a follow-up of earlier initiative. This holds true in particular in English, where during the German occupation itself the Ministry reemphasized the prewar program, devoting one (out of three) hours a week in the next-to-last class in the *lycée* to a quite extensive program of American Literature and Civilization. Even now, this plan is not being generally followed; there are too many practical difficulties. But this situation is fast improving as the new generation of teachers with more thorough American education takes its place in the schools. An impressive number of special editions of American authors and anthologies of "American Literature and Civilization" now exist for the *lycée*.

In the universities, American studies have been promoted since the war by several general reforms. A new introductory course (the *propédeutique*) was made compulsory for all students; and at intervals a number of universities have included subjects from American history, institutions, geography, economics, and "civilization" in these programs.

In the specialized study, American geography and history now tend to come in, on the various levels of examination,

by a rotation of three to five years. In English, the program
for the *agrégation* invariably lists two American authors out
of twelve for obligatory study; the candidate has to be able to
write an essay and give a public lecture, after five hours'
preparation, on any author in the program. In 1959 American requirements were also introduced in the second competitive examination, the CAPES. But the most important
innovation is a reform which made it possible to choose the
existing optional "Certificate of American Literature and
Civilization" as a part of the ordinary *licence* in English.
This reform was introduced in 1948; since then, fifteen of
the seventeen French universities have accepted this American certificate as a part of their programs, and about three-
fourths of all French candidates in English now pass it (at
the Sorbonne, between 80 and 90 per cent). The requirements
for the Certificate usually include the thorough *explication*
of a text chosen from a reading list of four to seven literary
works, and a broad program of knowledge in American Civilization.

Besides the chair of American Civilization at the Collège
de France there are now two full chairs of American literature at the Sorbonne alone and one chair of English and
American Language and Civilization, in addition to a lectureship. At the other universities, there are many similar
positions; and most important, numerous holders of general
chairs of English, history, and geography now have made the
teaching of American subjects a part of their ordinary duties.
Much of this work aims at the doctorate, where America
continues playing a considerable part in France; the Sorbonne
normally accepts about a dozen theses a year on American
subjects (one-third of them in Letters). Even outside the universities, French research in American studies after 1945

shows a broad approach which is paralleled only in Germany. There is a French journal for studies in English and American literature and language.

A somewhat different picture is again presented by Germany.

Postwar Germany in 1945 was in a state which seemed to prevent the establishment of any kind of creative order. There was terrible physical destruction, moral confusion, and intellectual bewilderment; and the country lacked any central authority, divided as it was between twelve *Länder* and four occupation zones. But this stage proved to be transitory. The Western powers adopted a policy basically different from that of 1918, and did their utmost to readmit Germany into the democratic world. Among the Germans themselves there was much willingness to co-operate both in political and cultural matters, and to begin afresh where the Weimar Republic had left off. In 1954 the occupation came to an end; the German Federal Republic was reorganized and accepted as a member of NATO, as "an experiment in good intentions and a hope for the future."

In this reconstruction, American studies came to play their part. The United States was predominant among the occupation powers; American authorities naturally tried to promote the study of their own civilization, and also to influence the work in the direction of integrated "area studies." These ideas did not lead to any broad reorganization in schools or universities. But even the Germans were now generally interested in giving American Civilization its share in German education; and in certain fields the "integrated" methods came to take on more importance than was the case elsewhere in Europe.

The German schools all had to be reorganized after the

war, and differences were considerable in the many independent *Länder*. Some efforts were made during this reorganization to introduce American studies as a separate subject, in
the spirit of the *Kulturkunde* of the 1920's. These efforts
all proved futile; instead, the *Länder*, in their new regulations,
strengthened American requirements in all individual subjects, and sometimes to a surprising extent. Quite a few of
these plans gave detailed directives for a concentrated American study in one special class. This planning was followed
up by a huge production of textbooks. In English alone, almost a hundred items were published especially for American
studies, and almost fifty separate editions appeared of American literary works, in addition to the great number of pages
alloted to the United States in general English anthologies.
As in France, the results in practice seem to be quite uneven
as yet, because the curricula are overcrowded; but compared
to the prewar situation progress has doubtless been considerable.

   In the universities there were strong demands for general
reform and for the introduction of new methods. Here
American studies played some part in the discussion. It was
suggested from the American side that a separate *Hochschule*
be established for "Americanistics" in order to serve as a
model of integrated studies. An effort in this direction was
actually made by the establishment with Rockefeller support
of the large American Institute in Munich, and related
problems were discussed in a number of conferences under
American auspices. The new methods met, however, with
much skepticism, as they did in the 1920's, and the conferences decided to allow each university to choose its own way.

   In practice this has meant that the most important university studies, those which take the student up to his school
examination, remain organized in the traditional subjects

as they always were. Only one university (in Mainz) has an optional examination in "Americanistics"; and even there, America is normally studied as a voluntary specialization within one of the ordinary disciplines. Most of the German *Länder* have generally strengthened American requirements at the examinations which qualify teachers for the secondary schools, but usually in somewhat vague terms. Under the German system this means that great discretionary power, now as before, is left with the full professor; often the development of American studies is still dependent on his personal favor, or lack of it.

These qualifications have not, however, prevented a striking growth of all kinds of American studies in postwar Germany. The best indicator remains the number of specialized courses which, during the first postwar decade, showed an average of almost four per university per semester (more than double the pre-1945 figure); only one-fourth of these courses were given by foreigners. There are about thirty teaching positions in West German universities the titles of which have direct reference to America, among them about a dozen full professorships.

This development is most striking in the field of American literature. A few German departments of English still largely disregard the subject. But the majority of the departments now more and more adopt the policy of making American material an obvious part of the study of English. An increasing number of universities, both large and small, have recently made basic American material compulsory for all English students on the lower level; thus, a further British or American specialization is almost equally attractive. Similarly, more and more universities now try to establish, beside the full chair of English, an "extraordinary" professorship "with special reference to American literature"; during the recent two years, such positions have been organized in four universities, and others are coming. As in France, much of American literature is also now being taught by the ordinary professors of English.

Interdisciplinary work is largely limited to studies for the doctorate, and is normally connected with the specialized American Institutes, of which Germany has six; a few of the American sections of the English Institutes would also well deserve that name. Some of these institutes are small, and quite traditional. Others base their work on a real co-operation of disciplines, organized in committees where all the pertinent branches of learning are represented. They allow for a great liberty of choice with regard to the subject and approach of a thesis; and no two of the institutes are alike, which makes for great variety in methods and instruction. There is no nation outside the United States today where the study of American Civilization shows so many facets and is so multifold in its scholarly organization as in present-day Germany.

This many-sidedness is expressed in independent research of great variety, and even in scholarly organization. There is an active German Association for American Studies, founded in 1953, and its annual yearbook (of which four volumes are in print) is by definition devoted to investigations which go beyond the limits of the individual discipline.

There is no reason to make a detailed survey of the present situation of American studies in all other countries of Western Europe. Largely speaking, there is the same unevenness which was found in the great powers, depending on the variety of nations, universities, and scholars; the same definite growth after the war, particularly in general requirements; and the same trend toward a more definite organization of the work.

Like the United Kingdom, Ireland has strong American history programs; and in 1953 the University of Dublin established the first optional American literature course. Among the neighbors of France, the Belgians still have a quite feeble system of American studies with a few optional and not very important literature courses; but some of the universities in French-speaking Switzerland are making good progress. Within the Germanic orbit the Dutch are gradually getting under way (there is an important American Institute in Amsterdam). But the leaders are Switzerland (particularly Zürich) and Austria. In the latter, American Civilization is today studied in carefully organized, compulsory courses from the secondary schools to the universities. At Vienna, since the war, a dozen specialized American courses have been offered annually, and the number of American literature theses for the doctorate is impressive. An American Institute was established in 1956 in Innsbruck.

The same development by steps can be followed in Scandinavia. Tiny Iceland, with its 160,000 souls, in 1957 received its first Fulbright lecturer in American studies. The University of Copenhagen in Denmark has a *Lektor* of American literature, and a full chair in the subject may be established in the foreseeable future. All the four universities of Sweden also have their American lectureships, and obligatory requirements are increasing, particularly at Uppsala. Oslo has had a full chair of American literature since 1946, and a good-sized selection of American texts is obligatory for all students of English. In Finland, suspended as it is between East and West but Western in its entire orientation, the two universities have impressive compulsory programs of the same kind. There are large American Institutes (mainly for literature) at Helsinki, Oslo, and Uppsala, and others are being developed at Copenhagen and Gothenburg. A Nordic Association for American Studies was founded in 1959.

This growth is often the result of a tug of war between many forces, a fact particularly striking in the Mediterranean region. Much could hardly be expected from the two dictatorships on the Iberian peninsula; nevertheless they show some progress, with characteristic differences. General Franco certainly has no idea of opening Spain to American influence; he has not even been willing to accept a Fulbright arrangement. But his military flirtation with the United States has induced him to some friendly gestures. Since 1953 a degree in modern languages in Madrid (the first degree of its kind in Spain) also includes courses in American literature, history, geography, and institutions that are compulsory for all students of English, and teaching is getting under way at a few universities. Among the theses of English in Madrid under the new degree almost one-third have had American subjects. Portugal's dictator, Salazar, on the other hand, is eager to cultivate the traditional Western relations of his country. Not a little American material was introduced into Portuguese secondary schools in 1948, and American institutes, with teaching on an optional basis, are now being developed at Coimbra and Lisbon.

Italy, an important NATO power, is increasingly developing its American studies. Difficulties are staggering; notwithstanding, definite progress has been made. Permanent optional courses of American literature and history are being established in quite a few universities, and recently, full American professorships (respectively in history, economics, government, and literature) have been organized in the universities of Florence, Genoa, Naples, and Rome. American research is impressive in Italy, particularly in literary criticism. Four volumes have appeared of the annual *Studi Americani;* and an Italian Association for American Studies was founded in 1958.

In the Roman Catholic nations of the western Mediterranean the approach to American studies has in many ways been hesitant, or even reluctant. The motley nations in the eastern parts of the region show a less ambiguous attitude, although for various reasons. Greece since 1952 has demonstrated its Western loyalty by a program of English in its two universities where three compulsory hours a week in the last year are devoted to America. Turkey, the military cornerstone of NATO in the Middle East, recently introduced a similar program in accordance with its continued policy of modernization. And Israel followed up about the same time, as part of its conscious effort to maintain the Western character of its culture against the onslaught of external enemies and the rising tide of Levantine immigration.

This schematic survey cannot be concluded without mentioning some efforts which are aiming at, or are typical of, the entire Western region of American studies in Europe.

Outside the framework of regular university studies a number of European countries have found it necessary since the war to organize special seminars or summer schools in American subjects. Some of these courses are highly specialized and are aimed at scholars and research workers; but most of them have reference to the new school regulations, and intend to answer the need of elementary and secondary school teachers for a more extensive knowledge of America. Such courses are at present being given more or less regularly in at least eight countries; in Italy these seminars may number about a dozen every year.

On the university level, great difficulties are presented everywhere in Europe by the uneven and scattered character of the holdings of American research material in libraries and archives. As a remedy, large-scale surveys are now being undertaken, primarily by the national Associations for American Studies, in order to co-ordinate information and make existing resources generally known. Union Catalogs of American books, periodicals, and newspapers are being worked on in a number of countries, and some of them are now appearing in print, above all the impressive Italian Catalog of Periodicals (1958). A *Guide to Manuscripts Relating to the United States in Great Britain and Ireland* was published in 1961; a similar German survey is finished and will be made available in xerographic reproduction.

Two European institutions are by definition organized for the promotion of American studies across national border lines. The Salzburg Seminar, through its thirteen years of existence, has given the initiation in American studies to more than three thousand European intellectuals, many of whom are now in some way or other connected with the subject. In co-operation with Johns Hopkins University, a European Center of American Studies was organized in 1960 in Bologna. The Center presents an ambitious program of specialized graduate study particularly of American history, political, social, and economic life. The Center is publishing the quarterly *American Review*.

The European Association for American Studies, founded in 1954, tries to co-ordinate all the scattered efforts through its annual *Newsletter* and its triennial European Conferences of American Studies.

We have made full circle; and in conclusion it is only too obvious how patchy is the picture which could be given. This survey took for its starting point the European mind as contrasted with the American myths in the work of schools and universities. But even within that framework less has been offered of the juice and life of American studies than of their bony educational skeleton, a mosaic of refractive details.

If these details have any justification, however, it is because they form part of a historic process of world dimensions. The growth of American studies in Europe is one aspect of that widening of the Old World's horizon which was initiated by Marco Polo and Christopher Columbus in the 14th and 15th centuries and was finally made evident to mankind in the 20th. The United States became a symbol of the new, global world, and of the forces that have molded it. The efforts of the Europeans to study America paralleled the growth of these forces and are indicative of their advance.

This fact implies that the development we have followed has been as motley as is Europe itself. Far from being concluded, the process is only in its beginning. Still it is hampered in manifold ways by traditionalism and bias; still the general results are often disproportionate to the significance of the subject. In 1950 the American High Commissioner for Germany, General J. J. McCloy, expressed the pious wish that American studies would someday be considered at German universities "just as important as Sanskrit and Egyptology." At about the same time a tabulation was made of specialized German university courses on the world cultures. In this list, American Civilization was still number fifteen; the nation was exactly on a level with Egypt but ranked far below India, Arabia, and China. With some modification, the same sobering picture would still appear today, in many European countries.

One cannot hope for any improvement in this situation overnight. There are still many factual difficulties, inherent both in the traditional educational systems and in the curiously mingled relationship of British and American civilizations. And there are natural limits to what one can expect from an American point of view. In Europe as in the United States itself it is the common Western heritage, back to the dawn of history, which will remain in the foreseeable future the cornerstone of education, and justly so.

But the educational atmosphere in Europe is changing. The series of psychological obstacles which long blocked the road of American studies in many European minds are fading away under the impact of the atomic era. The idea of an education for every man, focused on the problems of the modern world, has gained universal strength. It is being realized by more and more Europeans that even the values of tradition can only survive within an education of this type, and that American studies in European schools and universities, far from being a sign of submissiveness, are essential to the efforts of the Europeans to understand themselves.

In this light, the growth that is outlined in these chapters seems to hold high promise. The study on which this book is based, was begun in a spirit of protest against European negligence and complacency; it ended in a feeling of respect toward the degree of effort which these almost two hundred years of American studies involve, and in a mood of hopefulness about the future. It is encouraging to notice the variation, even the contradictions, within the field, and the spirit of experimentation which seems to adhere to it and which is in itself truly American. It is encouraging to follow the geographic expansion of the work, which makes it a focus of many civilizations and standards of life, from Lisbon to Moscow, from Helsinki to Jerusalem, and which in the long run is bound to influence the interplay of world cultures.

The future of these studies is veiled by the unforeseeable. It will depend on the position of the United States in the world, and on its spiritual power of leadership. It will depend, for quite some time to come, on American assistance; one hesitates to consider the future of American studies in Europe without a Fulbright program, or something like it, to span the gap of the ocean.

But the decisive factors will always be in Europe, as they were in the past—in the continued growth of realism and enlightened self-interest toward America in European minds. If American studies have continued strengthening their position through all these years, it is because they proved to be linked to basic problems in the life of modern man. They will have changed from the controversial to the obvious only when they are accepted as an indispensable part in the formation of Europe's destiny.

In the end, the future of American studies will thus depend on these studies themselves. In parts of Europe today American studies are made to serve preconceived ideas, while unpleasant facts are ignored or suppressed. In other countries too, including the United States itself, such tendencies can be found. If American studies are going to develop their potential strength, it will be because they live up to different ideals, and are able to demonstrate within their own orbit that quest for objective truth which links the noblest traditions of the Old World and the New.

Index of Names

Aberystwyth, 97
Åbo, 20, 104
Acton, Lord, 40
Adams, James Truslow, 91
Africa, 85
Alexander I, Emperor of
  Russia, 19
Alexander II, Emperor of
  Russia, 24
Alexander the Great, 25
Alps, 75
Amsterdam, 104
Anglo-Saxon, 46
Arabia, 85, 108
Arnold, Matthew, 25
Aryans, 77
Asia, 85, 87
Athens, 40
Atlantic, 23, 26, 39, 48,
  64, 84
Austria, 19, 23, 32, 53,
  79 f., 104

Bakunin, M., 24
Baldwin, Stanley, 62
Baltic, 56
Basel, 32
Belgium, 47, 104
Belgrade, 94
Bellamy, Edward, 39
Bellot, H. H., 64
Berkeley, Calif., 9
Berlin, 29 f., 44, 48 f., 69,
  78–81, 92
Bern, 32
Bismarck, Otto von, 49
Boewe, Charles and Mary,
  10
Bologna, 107
Bornhausen, Karl, 51
Bourgeois, Emile, 45
Brandenburg Gate, 91
Bratislava, 80
Bremen, 56
Bright, John, 32
British. See Great Britain.
Brogan, D. W., 64, 82
Bryce, James, 41, 57
Bucharest, 91
Burnett, Frances H., 49
Butler, R. A., 95

Caen, 46
California, 9
Cambridge (England), 40–
  42, 45, 64
Cather, Willa, 65
Catherine II, Empress of
  Russia, 17 f.
Celts, 52
Cestre, Charles, 45, 65, 81
Chamberlain, Joseph, 40
Charles X, King of France,
  26

Chateaubriand, F. R. de, 22
Chaucer, Geoffrey, 42
China, 30, 108
Christiania. See Oslo.
Churchill, Winston, 95
Clarendon Educational Re-
  port, 39
Cobden, Richard, 32
Coimbra, 105
Columbus, Christopher, 26,
  108
Constantinople, 84
Copenhagen, 31, 104 f.
Cornell University, 33
Crèvecœur, J. H. St. J. de,
  6
Crosby, Bing, 85
Czechoslovakia, 23, 53, 80,
  93

D'Annunzio, Gabriele, 54
Decembrists, 24
Denmark, 31, 104 f.
Dickens, Charles, 89
Dieppe, 98
Doll, Eugene, E., 8
Dreiser, Theodore, 91
Dublin, 104
Dutch. See Holland.

Ebeling, Christoph, 21 f.
Edinburgh, 40
Egypt, 108
Eliot, T. S., 22, 97
Emerson, Ralph Waldo, 46,
  91
Engels, F., 72, 88
England, English. See Great
  Britain.
Estonia, 79
Eton, 25 f., 63

Fast, Howard, 91
Fay, Bernard, 81
Fazy, James, 31
Ferdinand II, King of
  Naples, 24
Ferrero, Guglielmo, 54
Finland, 20, 104 f.
Florence, 106
France, 6, 17–19, 21 f., 24,
  26–28, 31, 33 f., 36, 42–
  51, 53 f., 57, 61, 64–66,
  69 f., 81, 84, 93, 98–100,
  103 f.
Franco, Francisco, 105
Franklin, Benjamin, 17, 19,
  33, 47, 49
Franklin Library (Paris), 45
Freiburg, 56
Fulbright, J. W., 104 f.,
  110

Garibaldi, G., 24

Gay, H. Nelson, 74 f.
Geneva, 20, 31
Genoa, 106
George, Henry, 39
Germanic, 104
Germany, 8, 20–22, 24,
  27–32, 37, 39, 41–44,
  46–53, 56, 61, 66–70,
  74–82, 84, 89, 91–93,
  98, 100–103, 107 f.
Glasgow, 42
Gorky, Maxim, 89
Gothenburg, 105
Göttingen, 21, 24, 32, 69,
  78
Grahame, James, 26
Grant, Madison, 77
Great Britain (British, Eng-
  lish, England, United
  Kingdom), 8, 15 f., 19 f.,
  22, 24–29, 31 f., 34,
  36–47, 49–55, 57, 62–
  64, 66–68, 70, 73, 75 f.,
  78, 82, 84, 86, 89, 91–
  93, 95–107, 109
Greece (Greek), 23, 32,
  37, 43, 54, 84, 106
Guiana (British), 63

Halle, 21
Hamburg, 48, 69
Harmsworth Chair, 64
Harrow, 25
Harvard University, 21 f.,
  40, 68
Hauser, Henri, 45
Haymarket Anarchists, 35
Heidelberg, 32
Heindel, Richard H., 39
Helsinki, 104 f., 110
Henry IV, King of France,
  34
Herder, J. G. von, 18
Herrig, L., 28 f.
Herzen, Aleksandr, 24
Hitler, Adolf, 69, 77, 80,
  82
Holland (Netherlands), 7,
  30, 104
Hollywood, 63
Holst, Hermann von, 56 f.
Hungary, 23, 91, 93 f.

Iberian Peninsula, 105 f.
Iceland, 104
India, 30, 108
Innsbruck, 104
Ireland, 57, 104, 107
Irving, Washington, 25, 29,
  49
Israel, 106
Italy, 19, 24, 53–55, 74–
  77, 82, 105–107

111